Winged Words

As darting swallows skim across a pool,
   Whose tranquil depths reflect a tranquil sky,
So, o'er the depths of silence, dark and cool,
   Our winged words dart playfully,
      And seldom break
   The quiet surface of the lake,
      As they flit by.

MARY COLERIDGE

WINGED WORDS

AN ANTHOLOGY OF VICTORIAN WOMEN'S POETRY AND VERSE

Compiled and introduced by
Catherine Reilly
with a preface by
Germaine Greer

ENITHARMON PRESS LONDON 1994

First published in 1994
by the Enitharmon Press
36 St George's Avenue
London N7 0HD

Distributed in Europe
by Password (Books) Limited
23 New Mount Street
Manchester, M4 4DE

Distributed in the USA
by Dufour Editions Inc.
PO Box 449, Chester Springs
PA 19425

ISBN 1 870612 24 8

The text is set in 10pt Bembo
by Bryan Williamson, Frome
and is printed in an edition of 2000 copies
by The Cromwell Press, Melksham, Wiltshire

To the Memory of My Beloved Grandmother,
Helena Macaulay, born a Victorian

ACKNOWLEDGEMENTS

I am most grateful to those who have helped me, in various ways, to complete this work. My thanks are due to Mary and Victor Schwarz for their encouragement at the start of the project; to Alice Lock, Local History Librarian, Tameside, John Thorn, Divisional Librarian, Portsmouth, and Ann MacEwan, all of whom assisted with biographical details on certain poets; to Jane Sellars, Director of the Brontë Parsonage Museum, for selecting the illustrations; to Deborah Forbes; and to Anne Harvey, good friend and 'anthologist extraordinary', for her sound advice and constant support.

C.R.

IMAGES IN THE TEXT

Chosen by Jane Sellars
Director of the Brontë Parsonage Museum, Haworth

CONTENTS

PREFACE

When Victoria ascended the throne in 1837, most women could read and write, but only an intrepid few dared to express themselves in verse. Verse was no longer to be practised as a mere accomplishment, for poetry had become the highest human calling, conferring virtually superhuman stature on its practitioners. Though good light verse, burlesque and satire were still being written, the figure that brooded over the literary landscape was not the Byron of *Don Juan* but the Byron of *Childe Harold*. As the author of *Childe Harold* Byron was as conspicuous a figure as the multi-million-seller pop star would be today, and the most deeply affected segment of his readership was female.

Victorian women poets were aware of themselves as daring adventurers, with a duty to reveal women's deepest emotional reality. They saw themselves as committed to the cause of the wordless and downtrodden; they wrote on behalf of children, beggars and cripples and of the outcast and the sinful. They wrote of the death of children and of the longing of the increasing proportion of women who were doomed never to find sexual love and never to marry. Some of their self-consciously poetic vocabulary might strike us today as false, but standards of contemporary taste demanded that the concerns of the uneducated be expressed in a language that transcended a particular time and a particular place.

The queen was herself a patron of women's artistic endeavour, as well as a conspicuously successful wife and mother. As the empire grew in extent, power and wealth, women began to exert more pressure on all parts of the establishment, in search of fuller participation. The poems in this collection show how they began to mock conventional pieties, to assert an independent questing sexuality, to protest against all kinds of inequality, of sex, race and class. Tennyson, Victoria's laureate and the greatest male poet of the epoch, was a deeply troubled man. Conventional piety had taken a blow from the new science; a new and terrible doubt about God's role in the world was threatening the optimism of thinking people in a terrifying way. The women poets, who had never shared in the bland certainties of the earlier era, addressed the problem in two ways, either by asserting the personal nature of their faith or by enacting their anxiety, even their despair.

By the time the great queen died in 1901 women had been clamouring for the right to honourable and satisfying work outside the home for many years. The struggle for women's right to vote was almost won. Having learnt how to organise and how to exercise a degree of power, women realised that women's contribution could not and should not be circumscribed by loyalty and obedience. The work of Florence Nightingale had shown that nurturance needs to be properly organised and managed; a whole generation of 'new' women were engaged in government projects to improve the health and happiness of the nation. The first female university graduates had shown that hard and prolonged study did not exhaust the female constitution or drive women out of their minds. Women stood on the brink of the longest revolution, their hearts and minds bent upon giving shape to an ideal of social justice the world has yet to see. The long centuries of silence were at an end.

Germaine Greer

INTRODUCTION

This anthology contains poems by sixty-eight Victorian women. A few, such as Elizabeth Barrett Browning, Emily Brontë and Christina Rossetti, have been recognized as major poets since the last century; their poetry has been analysed and commented upon in many works of criticism and in many biographies. Some, like Mary Coleridge, Michael Field, Jean Ingelow and Alice Meynell, have attracted favourable literary attention only comparatively recently, while a few, notably George Eliot and Edith Nesbit, are much better known in other areas of literature – Eliot as a major novelist, Nesbit as a writer of children's stories. In fact, the majority of contributors were writing in forms other than poetry, and were published regularly in magazines and newspapers. Some of the names will be familiar to students of the period but most will be unknown to the general reader.

Most were of English origin but nine were Irish, six were Scottish, two, Louise Imogen Guiney and Rosamund Marriott Watson, were born in the United States but had settled in England, while one, Mathilde Blind, was born in Germany.

They came from all strata of Victorian society but most were middle class. Seven were from the aristocracy – the titled landed gentry: Eva Gore-Booth, Harriet Eleanor Hamilton King, Lucy Knox, Emily Lawless, Caroline Lindsay, Emmeline Stuart-Wortley, and Grace Tollemache; six married into titled families or had a husband who was subsequently given a title: Olive Custance, Helen Selina Dufferin, Ann Hawkshaw, Rosa Mulholland, Caroline Norton, and Jane Francesca Wilde.

One or two interesting connections emerge: there are two sisters, Helen Selina Dufferin and Caroline Norton; an aunt and niece, Katherine Bradley and Edith Cooper, writing under the pseudonym Michael Field; and, most intriguingly, a connection with Oscar Wilde – Jane Francesca Wilde, Wilde's mother, is included, as is Olive Custance, who was later to marry Lord Alfred Douglas.

As with all anthologies this selection demonstrates the editor's personal taste. However, my choice has been particularly wide as, in the course of bibliographical research into general Victorian poetry, I have had the opportunity to visit the national copyright libraries in search of Victorian editions of virtually unknown poets, and have examined literally thousands of volumes.* The present collection is a 'by-product' of this research.

Anthologists are often accused of inadequate research. There are undoubtedly occasions where personal circumstances or pressure of time have prevented them from going to the library shelves to seek good material that may have been overlooked or forgotten. Perhaps they may add an occasional item found by chance on their own bookshelves but generally it appears they have based their collections on previously published anthologies, thus perpetuating the reputation of certain minor poets, often elevating them to an undeservedly high status.

Women poets are overshadowed by their male counterparts even in the most highly regarded anthologies. *The Oxford Book of Victorian Verse*, edited by Sir Arthur Quiller-Couch in 1912, includes only 42 women from a total of 272 poets; *The New Oxford Book of Victorian Verse*, edited by Christopher Ricks in 1987, includes only 21 women from a total of 112 poets. The same disproportion occurs in every general anthology of Victorian verse, without exception. The reasons for this neglect of women's writing, a neglect that also extends to forms of literature other than poetry, are varied and complex, not least the fact that the English literary tradition is predominantly male. A great deal of research into literature by women is now carried out in universities since the establishment of 'Women's Studies' departments, and this will help to redress the balance.

My choice of poems is based on several criteria. I have endeavoured to bring together a variety of themes and of literary styles. All the poems are intelligent, have something to say, and say it with great sincerity. Tragedy and humour are here, although humour was difficult to find amid the Victorian earnestness. Some poems have been chosen because they typify the kind of verse popular in the period, others because they portray various aspects of women's lives at that time.

Many of the poets were women of courage. All seemed aware of the prevailing social injustices. Some were much involved in good works of a philanthropic nature: Adelaide Ann Procter became ill as a result of her efforts in this regard. Dinah Maria Craik and Sarah Williams devoted part of their income to writers less fortunate than themselves. Many were leading figures in social reform: Eva Gore-Booth was active in the women's suffrage movement; Mary Howitt campaigned against slavery; Caroline Norton's battle for custody of her three sons helped change the law in women's favour; Fanny Parnell was actively involved in Land League agitation and in Irish politics generally; Elizabeth Wordsworth was the founder of two Oxford women's colleges.

The topics of the poems are many and various: the eternal facts of birth and death, love and friendship, family relationships, work and leisure, war and peace, nature and the seasons, the countryside and the town have all been treated with perception and sensitivity. I hope that the contents of this volume will add something to the received view of Victorian women's poetry and verse, and that the reader will find much to enjoy.

Catherine Reilly

---

* *Late Victorian Poetry, 1880-1899. A Bibliography*. Mansell Publishing, 1994. (First of three volumes).

CECIL FRANCES ALEXANDER

(1818-95)

Born in County Wicklow, Ireland, the second daughter of John Humphreys, a major in the Royal Marines. She began to write verse at the age of nine but is best known for her hymns, which include 'All Things Bright and Beautiful' and 'Once in Royal David's City'. With her friend Lady Harriet Howard, daughter of the Earl of Wicklow, she came under the influence of the Oxford Movement and published a series of tracts that first appeared in 1842. In 1850 she married the Rev. William Alexander, Rector of Termonamongan in Tyrone, who later became Bishop of Derry and subsequently Archbishop of Armagh. Her life was devoted to charitable works but she delighted in congenial company. She had two sons and two daughters.

The Beggar Boy

When the wind blows loud and fearful,
   And the rain is pouring fast,
And the cottage matron careful
   Shuts her door against the blast;

When lone mothers as they hearken,
   Think of sailor sons at sea,
And the eve begins to darken
   While the clocks are striking three;

When the pavement echoes only
   Now and then to passing feet;
Still the beggar boy goes lonely,
   Up and down the empty street.

On his brow the wet hair bristles,
   And his feet are blue with cold,
And the wind at pleasure whistles
   Through his garments torn and old.

You can hear the plaint he utters,
   Standing dripping at your door,
Through the splashing in the gutters,
   When the wind has lulled its roar.

Little children playing gladly,
 In the parlour bright and warm,
Look out kindly, look out sadly
 On the beggar in the storm.

Speak ye softly to each other,
 Standing by the window pane;
'Had he father, had he mother,
 Would they leave him in the rain?

'In our home is peace and pleasure,
 We are loved and cared about,
We must give from our full measure,
 To the wanderer without.'

In the Distance

In the distance, O my lady,
 Little lady, turned of three!
Will the woodland seem as shady?
 Will the sunshine seem as free?
Will the primrose buds come peeping
 Quite as bright beneath the tree?
And the brook sing in its leaping
 As they do for you and me?

O my darling, O my daisy,
 In the days that are to be,
In the distance dim and hazy
 With its lights far out at sea;
When you're tall and fair and stately,
 Will you ever care for me?
Will you prize my coming greatly
 As you did when you were three?

JOANNA BAILLIE
(1762-1851)

Born in Bothwell, Lanarkshire, the daughter of a Presbyterian minister who later became Professor of Divinity at Glasgow. Her brother was the distinguished anatomist Matthew Baillie. She received a good education in Glasgow, then in 1783 went to London where her brother was established as a physician. In 1791 she moved to Hampstead, remaining there for the rest of her life, living with her sister Agnes after their mother's death in 1806. A dramatist and poet, she enjoyed popular acclaim together with the esteem and affection of her literary contemporaries. Sir Walter Scott became a lifelong friend.

Hay-Making

Upon the grass no longer hangs the dew;
Forth hies the mower with his glittering scythe,
In snowy shirt bedight, and all unbraced,
He moves athwart the mead with sideling bend.
And lays the grass in many a swathy line;
In every field, in every lawn and mead,
The rousing voice of industry is heard;
The haycock rises, and the frequent rake
Sweeps on the fragrant hay in heavy wreaths.
The old and young, the weak and strong are there,
And, as they can, help on the cheerful work.
The father jeers his awkward half-grown lad,
Who trails his tawdry armful o'er the field,
Nor does he fear the jeering to repay.
The village oracle and simple maid
Jest in their turns and raise the ready laugh;
All are companions in the general glee;
Authority, hard favoured, frowns not there.
Some, more advanced, raise up the lofty rick,
Whilst on its top doth stand the parish toast
In loose attire and swelling ruddy cheek.
With taunts and harmless mockery she receives
The tossed-up heaps from fork of simple youth,
Who, staring on her, takes his arm away,
While half the load falls back upon himself.
Loud is her laugh, her voice is heard afar:
The mower busied on the distant lawn,

The carter trudging on his dusty way,
The shrill sound know, their bonnets tossed in air,
And roar across the field to catch the notice:
She waves her arm to them, and shakes her head,
And then renews her work with double spirit.
Thus do they jest and laugh away their toil,
Till the bright sun, now past its middle course,
Shoots down his fiercest beams which none may brave.
The stoutest arm feels listless, and the swart
And brawny-shouldered clown begins to fail.
But to the weary, lo – there comes relief!
A troop of welcome children, o'er the lawn,
With slow and wary steps approach: some bear
In baskets, oaten cakes or barley scones,
And gusty cheese and stoups of milk or whey:
Beneath the branches of a spreading tree,
Or by the shady side of the tall rick,
They spread their homely fare, and seated round,
Taste every pleasure that a feast can give.

ISABELLA BANKS

(1821-97)

Born in Manchester into an affluent home, the daughter of James Varley, a chemist with a business in Marriott's Court. She supported her father in his political work, becoming a member of the ladies' committee of the Anti-Corn Law League. A schoolmistress at Cheetham, north Manchester, she was a novelist, poet and contributor to leading magazines. In 1846 she married George Linnaeus Banks, the journalist, poet and orator, and assisted him in his journalistic work. Her best known novel *The Manchester Man*, depicting Manchester in the early nineteenth century, was serialized in *Cassell's Magazine* and first published in book form in 1876.

Who Are 'The People'?

The rogues who drink, and fight, and curse,
Who take a life to steal a purse,
Still driving on from bad to worse?
    These cannot be the People!
Who beat their women, miscalled wives,
And, foul with crime that never thrives,
Blot love from out their children's lives?
    These roughs are not the People!

The dainty fops who stroll the Mall,
Or idly haunt boudoir and ball,
The club, the Row, the opera-stall?
    Loungers are not the People!
The worse than fops who spend the night
In vices which profane the light,
And think indulgence theirs by right?
    Roués are not the People!

All they of deft or horny hand
Who in the mill or workshop stand,
Or dig our mines, or till our land; –
    Say, are not these the People?
All they who strive with heart and will
Their humble duty to fulfil,
And earn an honest living still; –
    Sure, these must be the People?

Nay; – they who toil with hands alone,
To forge our metal, hew our stone –
Merely machines of flesh and bone –
Can but be half a People!
But they – whate'er their class or state –
Whose minds control, whose minds create,
Whose hands and heads make nations great;
These thinkers are the People!

Yes, – they who work, and they who plan
To elevate and better man,
Conjoined may press into the van
And say, 'We are the People!'
But mere brute force, mere wealth, mere birth,
Cannot regenerate the earth;
'Tis thought *and* action, work *and* worth,
Combined, that make a People!

LOUISA SARAH BEVINGTON
(1845-)

A freethinker, poet, and essayist on evolutionary science. Charles Darwin is said to have admired her volume of poems *Key Notes*, published in 1876. She contributed articles to various periodicals, including *Nineteenth Century*, *Progress*, and *Liberty*, the latter a journal of anarchist communism. Occasionally she used the pseudonym Arbor Leigh. She married a Munich artist named Guggenberger, and moved to Germany in 1883.

Love and Language

Love that is alone with love
   Makes solitudes of throngs;
Then why not songs of silences, –
   Sweet silences of songs?

Parts need words: the perfect whole
   Is silent as the dead;
When I offered you my soul
   Heard you what I *said*?

The Secret of the Bees

How have you managed it? bright busy bee!
You are all of you useful, yet each of you free.

What man only talks of, the busy bee does;
Shares food, and keeps order, with no waste of buzz.

No cell that's too narrow, no squandering of wax,
No damage to pay, and no rent, and no tax.

No drones kept in honey to look on and prate,
No property tyrants, no big-wigs of State.

Free access to flowers, free use of all wings;
And when bee-life is threatened, then free use of stings.

No fighting for glory, no fighting for pelf;
Each thrust at the risk of each soldier himself.

Comes over much plenty one summer, you'll see
A lull and a leisure for each busy bee.

No over-work, under-work, glut of the spoil;
No hunger for any, no purposeless toil.

Economy, Liberty, Order, and Wealth! –
Say, busy bee, how you reached Social Health?

(Answer)

Say, rather, why *not*? It is easier so;
We have all the world open to come and to go.

We haven't got masters, we haven't got money,
We've nothing to hinder the gathering of honey.

The sun and the air and the sweet summer flowers
Attract to spontaneous use of our powers.

Our work is all natural – nothing but play,
For wings and proboscis can go their own way.

We find it convenient to live in one nest,
None hindering other from doing her best.

We haven't a Press, so we haven't got lies,
And it's worth no one's while to throw dust in our eyes.

We haven't among us a single pretence,
And we got our good habits through sheer Common-Sense.

MATHILDE BLIND

(1841-96)

Born in Mannheim, Germany, the daughter of a banker named Cohen. She subsequently adopted the name of her stepfather, Karl Blind. Blind, exiled from Germany for involvement with the 1849 Baden insurrection, brought his family to London, where Mathilde received an English education. She was, nevertheless, greatly influenced by the foreign refugees who frequented her stepfather's house. The continental connections she maintained throughout her life gave her literary work a cosmopolitan character. She wrote workmanlike biographies of George Eliot and Madame Roland, and translated the journal of Marie Bashkirtseff. She lived in Manchester for a time, enjoying the friendship of the painter Ford Madox Brown and his wife. In later life, in failing health, she travelled extensively in Italy and Egypt. She died in London, bequeathing the greater part of her estate to Newnham College, Cambridge.

Apple-Blossom

Blossom of the apple trees!
   Mossy trunks all gnarled and hoary,
   Grey boughs tipped with rose-veined glory,
Clustered petals soft as fleece
Garlanding old apple trees!

How you gleam at break of day!
   When the coy sun, glancing rarely,
   Pouts and sparkles in the pearly
Pendulous dewdrops, twinkling gay
On each dancing leaf and spray.

Through your latticed boughs on high,
   Framed in rosy wreaths, one catches
   Brief kaleidoscopic snatches
Of deep lapis-lazuli
In the April-coloured sky.

When the sundown's dying brand
   Leaves your beauty to the tender
   Magic spells of moonlight splendour,
Glimmering clouds of bloom you stand,
Turning earth to fairyland.

Cease, wild winds, O, cease to blow!
  Apple-blossom, fluttering, flying,
  Palely on the green turf lying,
Vanishing like winter snow;
Swift as joy to come and go.

from *Love in Exile*

Many will love you; you were made for love;
For the soft plumage of the unruffled dove
  Is not so soft as your caressing eyes.
You will love many; for the winds that veer
Are not more prone to shift their compass, dear,
  Than your quick fancy flies.

Many will love you; but I may not, no;
Even though your smile sets all my life aglow,
  And at your fairness all my senses ache.
You will love many; but not me, my dear,
Who have no gift to give you but a tear
  Sweet for your sweetness' sake.

Manchester by Night

O'er this huge town, rife with intestine wars,
Whence as from monstrous sacrificial shrines
Pillars of smoke climb heavenward, Night inclines
Black brows majestical with glimmering stars.
Her dewy silence soothes life's angry jars:
And like a mother's wan white face, who pines
Above her children's turbulent ways, so shines
The moon athwart the narrow cloudy bars.

Now toiling multitudes that hustling crush
Each other in the fateful strife for breath,
And, hounded on by divers hungers, rush
Across the prostrate ones that groan beneath,
Are swathed within the universal hush,
As life exchanges semblances with death.

EMILY BRONTË

(1818-48)

One of the daughters of Patrick Brontë, a clergyman of Irish descent who became rector of Haworth, Yorkshire, in 1820. His wife died of cancer in 1821, and his children were brought up by their aunt Elizabeth. Emily was sent to a boarding school for clergymen's daughters at Cowan Bridge with her elder sisters, two of whom, Maria and Elizabeth, died of tuberculosis in 1825. Between 1837 and 1838 she became a governess at Halifax, and in 1842 went with her sister Charlotte to teach at the Pensionat Heger in Brussels. Unable to stand the drudgery and restriction of life as a teacher, she returned home after nine months and remained in Haworth for the rest of her life. Her poems, together with those of Charlotte and Anne, were first published in 1846 under the pseudonyms of Currer, Ellis and Acton Bell. Emily, regarded by many as the greatest genius of the three sisters, was the most spirited in temperament. Her single novel *Wuthering Heights* is one of the classic works in the English language.

Fall, Leaves, Fall

Fall, leaves, fall; die, flowers, away;
Lengthen night and shorten day;
Every leaf speaks bliss to me
Fluttering from the autumn tree.
I shall smile when wreaths of snow
Blossom where the rose should grow;
I shall sing when night's decay
Ushers in a drearier day.

O Thy Bright Eyes Must Answer Now

O thy bright eyes must answer now,
When Reason, with a scornful brow,
Is mocking at my overthrow;
O thy sweet tongue must plead for me
And tell why I have chosen thee!

Stern Reason is to judgement come
Arrayed in all her forms of gloom;
Wilt thou my advocate be dumb?
No, radiant angel, speak and say
Why I did cast the world away;

Why have I persevered to shun
The common paths that others run;
And on a strange road journeyed on
Heedless alike of Wealth and Power –
Of Glory's wreath and Pleasure's flower.

These once indeed seemed Beings divine,
And they perchance heard vows of mine
And saw my offerings on their shrine –
But, careless gifts are seldom prized,
And mine were worthily despised;

So with a ready heart I swore
To seek their altar-stone no more,
And gave my spirit to adore
Thee, ever present, phantom thing –
My slave, my comrade, and my King!

A slave because I rule thee still;
Incline thee to my changeful will
And make thy influence good or ill –
A comrade, for by day and night
Thou art my intimate delight –

My Darling Pain that wounds and sears
And wrings a blessing out from tears
By deadening me to real cares;
And yet, a king – though prudence well
Have taught thy subject to rebel.

And am I wrong to worship where
Faith cannot doubt nor Hope despair
Since my own soul can grant my prayer?
Speak, God of Visions, plead for me
And tell why I have chosen thee!

'Often Rebuked'

Often rebuked, yet always back returning
  To those first feelings that were born with me,
And leaving busy chase of wealth and learning
  For idle dreams of things which cannot be:

To-day, I will seek not the shadowy region;
  Its unsustaining vastness waxes drear;
And visions rising, legion after legion,
  Bring the unreal world too strangely near.

I'll walk, but not in old heroic traces,
  And not in paths of high morality,
And not among the half-distinguished faces,
  The clouded forms of long-past history.

I'll walk where my own nature would be leading:
  It vexes me to choose another guide:
Where the gray flocks in ferny glens are feeding;
  Where the wild wind blows on the mountain side.

What have those lonely mountains worth revealing?
  More glory and more grief than I can tell:
The earth that wakes *one* human heart to feeling
  Can centre both the worlds of Heaven and Hell.

The Old Stoic

Riches I hold in light esteem,
And Love I laugh to scorn;
And lust of Fame was but a dream
That vanished with the morn –

And if I pray, the only prayer
That moves my lips for me
Is – 'Leave the heart that now I bear,
And give me liberty.'

Yes, as my swift days near their goal,
'Tis all that I implore –
Through life and death, a chainless soul,
With courage to endure!

Tell Me, Tell Me, Smiling Child

Tell me, tell me, smiling child,
What the past is like to thee?
'An Autumn evening soft and mild
With a wind that sighs mournfully.'

Tell me, what is the present hour?
'A green and flowery spray
Where a young bird sits gathering its power
To mount and fly away.'

And what is the future, happy one?
'A sea beneath a cloudless sun;
A mighty, glorious, dazzling sea
Stretching into infinity.'

The Visionary

Silent is the house: all are laid asleep:
One alone looks out o'er the snow-wreaths deep,
Watching every cloud, dreading every breeze
That whirls the wildering drift, and bends the groaning trees.

Cheerful is the hearth, soft the matted floor;
Not one shivering gust creeps through pane or door;
The little lamp burns straight, its rays shoot strong and far:
I trim it well, to be the wanderer's guiding-star.

Frown, my haughty sire! chide, my angry dame;
Set your slaves to spy; threaten me with shame:
But neither sire nor dame, nor prying serf shall know,
What angel nightly tracks that waste of frozen snow.

What I love shall come like visitant of air,
Safe in secret power from lurking human snare;
What loves me, no word of mine shall e'er betray,
Though for faith unstained my life must forfeit pay.

Burn, then, little lamp; glimmer straight and clear –
Hush! a rustling wing stirs, methinks, the air:
He for whom I wait, thus ever comes to me;
Strange Power! I trust thy might; trust thou my constancy.

MARY ANNE BROWNE
(1812-44)

Born in Maidenhead, Berkshire. From 1830 to 1842 she lived most of the time in Liverpool, where her father had moved his business in 1829. She published several novels and was a frequent contributor to various British and American periodicals. In 1842 she married James Gray, a Scot. She died in Cork, Ireland.

The Embroideress at Midnight

She plies her needle till the lamp
  Is waxing pale and dim;
She hears the watchman's heavy tramp,
  And she must watch like him: –
Her hands are dry, her forehead damp,
  Her dark eyes faintly swim.

Look on her work! – here blossom flowers,
  The lily and the rose,
Bright as the gems of summer hours,
  But not to die like those;
Here, fadeless as in Eden's bowers,
  For ever they repose.

Once, maiden, thou wast fresh and fair
  As those sweet flowers of thine;
Now, shut from sunny light and air,
  How canst thou choose but pine?
Neglected flows thy raven hair,
  Like the uncultured vine.

Look on her work! – no common mind
  Arranged that glowing group –
Wild wreaths the stately roses bind,
  Sweet bells above them droop –
Ye almost *see* the sportive wind
  Parting the graceful troop!

Look on her work! – but look the more
  On her unwearied heart,
And put aside the chamber-door
  That doth the daughter part
From that dear mother, who before
  Taught her this cunning art.

She sleeps – that mother, sick and pale –
  She sleeps – and little deems
That she, who doth her features veil,
  All day, in flitting gleams
Of anxious hope, this hour doth hail,
  But not for happy dreams.

God bless her in her lone employ,
  And fill those earnest eyes
With visions of the coming joy,
  Waiting her sacrifice,
When they, who give her this employ,
  Pay her its stinted price!

ELIZABETH BARRETT BROWNING
(1806-61)

Born at Coxhoe Hall, Durham, eldest of the twelve children of Edward and Mary Moulton-Barrett. From 1809 to 1832 the family lived at Hope End, Ledbury, Herefordshire. After a period in Sidmouth, Mr Barrett moved his family to London in 1835. He became increasingly tyrannical, forbidding any of his children to marry. Largely self-educated, Elizabeth was an accomplished classical scholar although she suffered chronic ill-health, notably bronchitis. In London she led the sheltered and restricted life of an invalid, seldom leaving her room. The several volumes of poetry she published between 1826 and 1844 established her reputation, and there was serious talk of her becoming Poet Laureate. In 1844 she secretly married another rising poet, Robert Browning, and went to live in Italy where the climate improved her health. The Brownings settled first in Pisa, then in Florence, becoming the centre of a literary circle, while Elizabeth fervently supported the cause of Italian nationalism. Despite several miscarriages, in 1849 she gave birth to a healthy boy, Robert.

The Best Thing in the World

What's the best thing in the world?
June-rose, by May-dew impearl'd;
Sweet south-wind, that means no rain;
Truth, not cruel to a friend;
Pleasure, not in haste to end;
Beauty, not self-deck'd and curl'd
Till its pride is over-plain;
Light, that never makes you wink;
Memory, that gives no pain;
Love, when, *so*, you're loved again.
What's the best thing in the world?
– Something out of it, I think.

Grief

I tell you, hopeless grief is passionless;
   That only men incredulous of despair,
   Half-taught in anguish, through the midnight air
Beat upward to God's throne in loud access
Of shrieking and reproach. Full desertness,
   In souls as countries lieth silent-bare
   Under the blanching, vertical eye-glare
Of the absolute Heavens. Deep-hearted man, express
Grief for thy dead in silence like to death –
   Most like a monumental statue set
In everlasting watch and moveless woe
Till itself crumble to the dust beneath.
   Touch it; the marble eyelids are not wet:
If it could weep, it could arise and go.

Pain in Pleasure

A thought lay like a flower upon mine heart,
And drew around it other thoughts like bees
For multitude and thirst of sweetnesses;
Whereat rejoicing, I desired the art
Of the Greek whistler, who to wharf and mart
Could lure those insect swarms from orange-trees,
That I might hive with me such thoughts, and please
My soul so, always. Foolish counterpart
Of a weak man's vain wishes! While I spoke,
The thought I called a flower grew nettle-rough –
The thoughts, called bees, stung me to festering.
Oh, entertain (cried Reason, as she woke,)
Your best and gladdest thoughts but long enough
And they will prove sad enough to sting.

BEATRICI CENCI.

ENGRAVED BY W. ROFFE FROM THE SCULPTURE BY HARRIET HOSMER

XXIX

I think of thee! – my thoughts do twine and bud
About thee, as wild vines, about a tree,
Put out broad leaves, and soon there's nought to see
Except the straggling green which hides the wood.
Yet, O my palm-tree, be it understood
I will not have my thoughts instead of thee
Who art dearer, better! rather instantly
Renew thy presence. As a strong tree should,
Rustle thy boughs and set thy trunk all bare,
And let these bands of greenery which insphere thee,
Drop heavily down, .. burst, shattered, everywhere!
Because, in this deep joy to see and hear thee
And breathe within thy shadow a new air,
I do not think of thee – I am too near thee.

XXXV

If I leave all for thee, wilt thou exchange
And *be* all to me? Shall I never miss
Home-talk and blessing, and the common kiss
That comes to each in turn, nor count it strange,
When I look up, to drop on a new range
Of walls and floors . . . another home than this?
Nay, wilt thou fill that place by me which is
Filled by dead eyes too tender to know change?
That's hardest! If to conquer love, has tried,
To conquer grief tries more . . . as all things prove
For grief indeed is love and grief beside.
Alas, I have grieved so I am hard to love –
Yet love me – wilt thou? Open thine heart wide,
And fold within, the wet wings of thy dove.

XXXVIII

First time he kissed me, he but only kissed
The fingers of this hand wherewith I write,
And ever since it grew more clean and white...
Slow to world-greetings... quick with its 'Oh, list,'
When the angels speak. A ring of amethyst
I could not wear here plainer to my sight,
Than that first kiss. The second passed in height
The first, and sought the forehead, and half missed,
Half falling on the hair. O beyond meed!
That was the chrism of love, which love's own crown,
With sanctifying sweetness, did precede.
The third upon my lips was folded down
In perfect, purple state; since when, indeed,
I have been proud and said, 'My Love, my own.'

XLIV

Beloved, thou hast brought me many flowers
Plucked in the garden, all the summer through
And winter, and it seemed as if they grew
In this close room, nor missed the sun and showers.
So, in the like name of that love of ours,
Take back these thoughts which here unfolded too,
And which on warm and cold days I withdrew
From my heart's ground. Indeed, those beds and bowers
Be overgrown with bitter weeds and rue,
And wait thy weeding; yet here's eglantine,
Here's ivy! – take them, as I used to do
Thy flowers, and keep them where they shall not pine.
Instruct thine eyes to keep their colours true,
And tell thy soul, their roots are left in mine.

A Woman's Shortcomings

I

She has laughed as softly as if she sighed,
  She has counted six, and over,
Of a purse well filled, and a heart well tried –
  Oh, each a worthy lover!
They 'give her time'; for her soul must slip
  Where the world has set the grooving.
She will lie to none with her fair red lip –
  But love seeks truer loving.

II

She trembles her fan in a sweetness dumb,
  As her thoughts were beyond recalling,
With a glance for *one*, and a glance for *some*,
  From her eyelids rising and falling;
Speaks common words with a blushful air,
  Hears bold words, unreproving;
But her silence says – what she never will swear –
  And love seeks better loving.

III

Go, lady, lean to the night-guitar,
  And drop a smile to the bringer,
Then smile as sweetly, when he is far,
  At the voice of an indoor singer.
Bask tenderly beneath tender eyes;
  Glance lightly, on their removing;
And join new vows to old perjuries –
  But dare not call it loving.

IV

Unless you can think, when the song is done,
  No other is soft in the rhythm;
Unless you can feel, when left by One,
  That all men else go with him;
Unless you can know, when upraised by his breath,
  That your beauty itself wants proving;
Unless you can swear, 'For life, for death!' –
  Oh, fear to call it loving!

V

Unless you can muse in a crowd all day
  On the absent face that fixed you;
Unless you can love, as the angels may,
  With the breadth of heaven betwixt you;
Unless you can dream that his faith is fast,
  Through behoving and unbehoving;
Unless you can *die* when the dream is past –
  Oh, never call it loving!

Work and Contemplation

The woman singeth at her spinning-wheel
A pleasant chant, ballad or barcarolle;
She thinketh of her song, upon the whole,
Far more than of her flax; and yet the reel
Is full, and artfully her fingers feel
With quick adjustment, provident control,
The lines, too subtly twisted to unroll,
Out to a perfect thread. I hence appeal
To the dear Christian church – that we may do
Our Father's business in these temples murk,
Thus, swift, and steadfast; thus, intent and strong;
While, thus, apart from toil, our souls pursue
Some high, calm, spheric tune, and prove our work
The better for the sweetness of our song.

ADA CAMBRIDGE
(1844-1926)

Born at Wiggenhall, St Germains, Norfolk, second of the ten children of Henry and Thomasine Cambridge. Theirs was a devoutly Church of England household, and in 1870 she married George Frederick Cross, a young curate. They emigrated to Victoria, Australia, where Cross served as an Anglican minister in a succession of parishes, moving to Williamstown in 1893. Ada Cambridge wrote romantic novels and contributed stories to newspapers and magazines, probably to supplement family income. She is seen as the first Australian writer of prose or verse to be concerned with the socially disadvantaged. In England she was regarded as a radical, in Australia a conservative. She made visits to England in 1908 and 1917 but returned to Australia after her husband's death in 1917. Her sight failed badly in her last years.

A Street Riot

Poor, hapless souls! at whom we stand aghast,
    As at invading armies sweeping by –
    As strange to haggard face and desperate cry –
Did we not know the worm must turn at last?
Poor, hungry men, with hungry children cast
    Upon the wintry streets to thieve or die –
    Suffering your wants and woes so silently –
Patient so long – is all your patience past?

Are there no ears to hear this warning call?
    Are there no eyes to see this portent dread?
Must brute force rise and social order fall,
    Ere these starved millions can be clothed and fed?
Justice be judge. Let future history say
Which are the greatest criminals to-day.

ELIZABETH RACHEL CHAPMAN

(1827-96)

Born in Woodford, Essex, into a family originally from Whitby, Yorkshire. Connected both paternally and maternally with the Gurneys of Norwich, and lineally descended from Elizabeth Fry. She wrote fiction, essays and poetry, and was interested in the social and philanthropic movements of the day, particularly in those specially affecting women. Her prose works include *Why We Should Oppose Divorce*, 1890, and *Marriage Questions in Modern Fiction*, 1897.

A Little Child's Wreath

in memoriam R.M.

Our Roger loved the fields, the flowers, the trees;
Great London jarred him; he was ill at ease
And alien in the stir, the noise, the press;
The city vexed his perfect gentleness.

So, loving him, we sent him from the town
To where the autumn leaves were falling brown,
And the November primrose, pale and dim,
In his own garden-plot delighted him.

There, like his flowers, he would thrive and grow,
We in our fondness thought. But God said: No,
Your way is loving, but not wholly wise;
My way is best – to give him Paradise.

Turn where I will, I miss, I miss my sweet;
By my lone fire, or in the crowded way
Once so familiar to his joyous feet,
I miss, I hunger for him all the day.

This is the house wherefrom his welcome rang;
These are the wintry walks where he and I
Would pause to mark if a stray robin sang,
Or some new sunset-flame enriched the sky.

Here, where we crossed the dangerous road, and where
Unutterably desolate I stand,
How often, peering through the sombre air,
I felt the sudden tightening of his hand!

Round me the city looms, void, waste and wild,
Wanting the presence of one little child.

MARY COLERIDGE
(1861-1907)

Born in London. Her father, Arthur Duke Coleridge, was Clerk of the Assize on the Midland Circuit and a nephew of Samuel Taylor Coleridge. Mary was educated at home, partly by the poet William Johnson Cory. A novelist, essayist and poet, her literary reputation was established by *The King With Two Faces*, an historical romance published in 1897. She devoted much time to teaching working women in her own home and gave lessons in English literature at the Working Women's College. On publication her poems were praised by Binyon, Bridges, and Edward Thomas. Her work is often compared with that of her American contemporary Emily Dickinson. She was a close friend of Henry and Margaret Newbolt. She died at Harrogate, Yorkshire.

At First

The grief of age is not the grief of youth;
A child is still a child, even in his grieving.
Yet his first sorrow is, in very truth,
Dark, past believing,

When first he wanders forth in early spring,
Nor heeds among the flowers each gay newcomer,
When first he hates the happy birds that sing,
The sun that shines in summer.

A Clever Woman

You thought I had the strength of men,
Because with men I dared to speak,
And courted science now and then,
And studied Latin for a week;
But woman's woman, even when
She reads her Ethics in the Greek.

You thought me wiser than my kind;
  You thought me 'more than common tall';
You thought because I had a mind,
  That I could have no heart at all;
But woman's woman you will find,
  Whether she be great or small.

And then you needs must die – ah, well!
  I knew you not, you loved not me.
'Twas not because that darkness fell,
  You saw not what there was to see.
But I that saw and could not tell –
  O evil Angel, set me free!

Eyes

Eyes, what are they? Coloured glass,
Where reflections come and pass.

Open windows – by them sit
Beauty, Learning, Love, and Wit.

Searching cross-examiners;
Comfort's holy ministers.

Starry silences of soul,
Music past the lips' control.

Fountains of unearthly light;
Prisons of the infinite.

Gone

About the little chambers of my heart
Friends have been coming – going – many a year.
    The doors stand open there.
Some, lightly stepping, enter; some depart.

Freely they come and freely go, at will.
The walls give back their laughter; all day long
    They fill the house with song.
One door alone is shut, one chamber still.

'I Saw a Stable'

I saw a stable, low and very bare,
  A little child in a manger.
The oxen knew Him, had Him in their care,
  To men He was a stranger.
The safety of the world was lying there,
  And the world's danger.

No Newspapers

Where, to me, is the loss
  Of the scenes they saw – of the sounds they heard;
A butterfly flits across,
  Or a bird;
The moss is growing on the wall,
  I heard the leaf of the poppy fall.

Solo

Leave me alone! my tears would make you laugh,
Or kindly turn away to hide a smile.
My brimming granaries cover many a mile;
How should you know that all my corn is chaff?
Leave me alone! my tears would make you laugh.

Leave me alone! my mirth would make you weep.
I only smile at all that you hold dear;
I only laugh at that which most you fear;
I see the shallows where you sound the deep.
Leave me alone! my mirth would make you weep.

'Some in a Child Would Live'

Some in a child would live, some in a book;
   When I am dead let there remain of me
Less than a word – a little passing look,
Some sign the soul had once, ere she forsook
   The form of life to live eternally.

Winged Words

As darting swallows skim across a pool,
   Whose tranquil depths reflect a tranquil sky,
So, o'er the depths of silence, dark and cool,
   Our winged words dart playfully,
      And seldom break
   The quiet surface of the lake,
      As they flit by.

ELIZA COOK
(1818-89)

Born in Southwark, youngest of the eleven children of a brazier. When she was about nine years old her father retired and the family went to live at a small farm near Horsham, Sussex. Almost entirely self-educated, she began to write verse at an early age, her first volume *Lays of a Wild Harp* appearing in 1835 when she was seventeen. She contributed to many magazines and in 1849 brought out a periodical for family reading which she called *Eliza Cook's Journal*. It had wide popular appeal and was highly successful for a time but was discontinued in 1854 because of her poor health. She was compelled to take a long rest, and it was not until 1864 that her next work *New Echoes* was published. In 1863 she received a civil list pension of £100 a year. She became something of a confirmed invalid, and died at Thornton Hill, Wimbledon.

The Idiot-Born

'Out, thou silly moon-struck elf;
Back, poor fool, and hide thyself!'
This is what the wise ones say,
Should the Idiot cross their way:
But if we would closely mark
We should see him not *all* dark
We should find we must not scorn
The teaching of the Idiot-born.

He will screen the newt and frog;
He will cheer the famished dog;
He will seek to share his bread
With the orphan, parish fed:
He will offer up his seat
To the stranger's wearied feet:
Selfish tyrants, do not scorn
The teaching of the Idiot-born.

Use him fairly, he will prove
How the simple breast can love;
He will spring with infant glee
To the form he likes to see.
Gentle speech, or kindness done;
Truly binds the witless one.
Heartless traitors, do not scorn
The teaching of the Idiot-born.

He will point with vacant stare
At the robes proud churchmen wear;
But he'll pluck the rose, and tell,
God hath painted it right well.
He will kneel before his food,
Softly saying, 'God is good.'
Haughty prelates, do not scorn
The teaching of the Idiot-born.

Art thou great as man can be? –
The same hand moulded him and thee.
Hast thou talent? – Taunt and jeer
Must not fall upon his ear.
Spurn him not; the blemished part
Had better be the head than heart.
Thou wilt be the fool to scorn
The teaching of the Idiot-born.

from *The Room of the Household*

There's a room that I love dearly – the sanctum of bliss,
That contains all the comforts I least like to miss;
Where, like ants in a hillock, we run in and out,
Where sticks grace the corner, and hats lie about;
Where no idlers dare come to annoy or amuse
With their 'morning call' budget of scandalous news.
'Tis the room of the Household – the sacredly free –
'Tis the room of the Household that's dearest to me

The romp may be fearlessly carried on there,
No 'bijouterie' rubbish solicits our care;
All things are as meet for the hand as the eye,
And patchwork and scribbling unheeded may lie;
'Black Tom' may be perched on the sofa or chairs,
He may stretch his sharp talons and scatter his hairs;
Wet boots may 'come in', and the ink-drop may fall,
For the room of the Household is 'liberty hall'.

Other rooms may be rich in the gorgeous display
Of Murillos and Titians in boasted array:
But the Morland and Wilkie that hang on the wall
Of the family parlour, out-value them all.
The gay ottomans, claiming such special regard,
Are exceedingly fine, but exceedingly hard;
They may serve for state purpose – but go, if you please,
To the Household-room cushions for comfort and ease.

And the bookshelves – where tomes of all sizes are spread,
Not placed to be looked at, but meant to be read;
All defaced and bethumbed, and I would not be sworn,
But some volumes, perchance the most precious, are torn.
There's the library open; – but if your heart yearns,
As all human hearts must, for the song of a Burns,
Or the tale of a 'Vicar' – that ever rich gem, –
You must go to the room of the Household for them.

I've wandered far off, over 'moorland and lea',
O'er the fairest of earth and the bluest of sea;
It was health that I sought – but, alas! I could find
The pursuit was in vain while my heart looked behind.
The room of the Household had bound with a spell,
And I knew not till then that I loved it so well:
'Take me back to that room', was my prayer and my cry,
'For my languishing spirit does nothing but sigh'.

Song of the Modern Time

Oh, how the world has altered since some fifty years ago!
When boots and shoes would *really* serve to keep out rain and snow;
But double soles and broadcloth – oh, dear me, how very low,
To talk of such old-fashioned things! when every one must know
That we are well-bred gentlefolks, all of the modern time.

We all meet now at midnight-hour, and form a 'glittering throng,'
Where lovely angels polk and waltz, and chant a German song:
Where 'nice young men,' with fierce moustache, trip mincingly along,
And the name of a good, old country-dance would sound like a Chinese gong
In the ears of well-bred gentlefolks, all of the modern time.

Your beardless boys, all brag and noise, must 'do the thing that's right;'
That is, they'll drink champagne and punch, and keep it up all night:
They'll smoke and swear till, sallying forth at peep of morning light,
They knock down some old woman, just to show how well they fight;
Like brave, young, English gentlemen, all of the modern time.

At the good old hours of twelve and one our grandsires used to dine,
And quaff their horns of nut-brown ale and eat roast beef and chine;
But we must have our silver forks, ragouts, and foreign wine,
And not sit down till five or six, if we mean to 'cut a shine;'
Like dashing, well-bred gentlefolks, all of the modern time.

Our daughters now at ten years old must learn to squall and strum,
And study shakes and quavers under Signor Fee-Foo-Fum;
They'll play concertos, sing bravuras, rattle, scream, and thrum,
Till you almost wish that you were deaf, or they, poor things, were dumb;
But they must be like young gentlefolks, all of the modern time.

Our sons must jabber Latin verbs, and talk of a Greek root,
Before they've left off tunic skirts, cakes, lollypops, and fruit;
They all have 'splendid talents,' that the desk or bar would suit;
Each darling boy would scorn to be 'a low mechanic brute:'
They must be well-bred College 'men,' all of the modern time.

But bills will come at Christmas tide, alas! alack-a-day!
The creditors may call again, 'Papa's not in the way;
He's out of town, but certainly next week he'll call and pay;'
And then his name's in the 'Gazette;' and this I mean to say
  Oft winds up many gentlefolks, all of the modern time.

ELIZABETH CRAIGMYLE

Born at Strawberry Bank, Aberdeen, daughter of a scholar and bookman. She was educated at Aberdeen High School, and at St Andrews, Aberdeen and London Universities, and became a lecturer at Bishop Otter College, Chichester. A translator from the Greek, French, and German, she published an edition of Goethe's *Faust* in the 'Canterbury Poets' series.

Chained Tigers

I

There is a dreadful legend of the past,
  Tells how, for some love-crime, a wretched man
  Was dungeoned with a tiger Lybian,
Each in a corner of the cell bound fast,
Left face to face together, till at last
  Hunger should give the tiger strength to break
  The brazen links that bound him, and to make
The prisoner's quivering limbs his fell repast.

Did the man's ear at last strain for the rend
  Of breaking links that set the chained brute free?
  Did he at every instant seem to see
The tawny limbs curve for the gathered bound,
Feel foam-flecked jaws about his throat close round,
  Feel the white fangs gnash through and make an end?

II

My cell is narrower. Shut within a room
  Whose threshold I shall never cross again,
  I hear no echoes from the world of men,
Buried, as if already in the tomb.
To my sick brain familiar things assume
  Unholy shapes that haunt me all the day,
  Then, when night falls, on bat-wings flit away,
And leave more ghastly things to fill the gloom.

And ever, within spring-reach of my bed,
  Crouch the twin-tigers chained, Disease and Death,
  All day I hear the horror of their breath,
Their hot sighs with my laboured breathings blend,
  All night on me their hungry eyes burn red, –
  Ah God! when will they spring, and make an end?

My Bookcase

How many volumes do I miss!
  I wish, among folks' duties,
That they would rank returning books.
  But those morocco beauties
Are never touched except by me,
  And really, though I know it's
A shame, I do rejoice to think
  That no one borrows poets.

To those lost books my fancy clings,
  O'er them my memory grovels,
I swear in spirit when I see
  The gaps among the novels.
The Thackeray I 'loved and lost'
  I mourn with sorrow tender,
Whoever has it also has
  The curses of the lender.

The second shelf I frankly own
  A motley, queer collection,
Half-filled with grave philosophers,
  In spite of Kant's defection.
But Calverley and Kingsley sit
  Tucked in among the Germans,
And 'Ouida' snugly nestles next
  My only book of sermons.

Spencer keeps cheerful company
  With 'How I caught a Tartar',
Near them the book I treasure most,
  My well-beloved 'Sartor'.

Montgomery by Macaulay stands,
  The scorned beside the scorner,
And dear Mark Twain with Rabelais
  Is chatting in the corner.

Homer! This same old copy shone,
  Star of my childish vision;
To read it for myself was once
  The height of my ambition.
Full fifteen years ago I made
  That blot upon the binding,
Trying to print my name in Greek,
  And difficulty finding.

Dear books! your answer questioning
  Without a why or wherefore.
Our friendship never had a jar;
  You seem to know and care for
The tender touches that I give
  To every well-worn cover,
And as I love you, friends of mine,
  I could not have a lover.

Under Deep Apple Boughs

The garden-shadows are flecked with the glory of light.
  In the light, the tulips flame; in the dark, fern fronds uncurl;
And each red apple-bloom bursts its beauty into white,
  As if a ruby should break, and shatter into a pearl.

They flutter slowly downward, and fall, soft as a snow-shower,
  Here at our feet their loveliness finds an end.
Was it worth to make such beauty only for one hour?
  Do you grieve for the fate of the blossoms, O my friend?

When Autumn stands in the land, with full and bounteous bosom,
  Honey-sweet fruit shall hang, ripening and red on the wall.
Shall girlhood's gift of versing be but a barren blossom?
  Wait, heart. Thy fruit shall set, when the flowers of fancy fall.

DINAH MARIA CRAIK

(1826-87)

Born in Stoke-on-Trent, Staffordshire, daughter of Thomas Mulock, a Nonconformist clergyman. Her father supervised her education and encouraged her early efforts. She settled in London about 1846, at first writing children's books but later producing a series of successful novels, the best-known of which is *John Halifax, Gentleman*. She moved to Hampstead in 1859, and set aside a pension of £60 for authors less fortunate than herself. In 1865 she married George Lillie Craik, who became a partner in the publishing house of Alexander Macmillan. She took up residence at Shortlands, near Bromley, Kent, spending a period of quiet happiness and literary industry until her death from a heart attack in 1887.

A Dead Baby

Little soul, for such brief space that entered
   In this little body straight and chilly,
Little life that fluttered and departed,
   Like a moth from out a budding lily,
Little being, without name or nation,
Where is now thy place among creation?

Little dark-lashed eyes, that never opened,
   Little mouth, by earthly food ne'er tainted,
Little breast, that just once heaved, and settled
   To eternal slumber, white and sainted, –
Child, shall I in future children's faces
See some pretty look that thine retraces?

Is this thrill that strikes across my heart-strings
   And in dew beneath my eyelid gathers,
Token of the bliss thou mightst have brought me,
   Dawning of the love they call a father's?
Do I hear through this still room a sighing
Like thy spirit to me its author crying?

SPRING

Whence didst come and whither take thy journey,
Little soul, of me and mine created?
Must thou lose us, and we thee, forever,
O strange life, by minutes only dated?
Or new flesh assuming, just to prove us,
In some other babe return and love us?

Idle questions all: yet our beginning
Like our ending, rests with the Life-sender,
With whom naught is lost, and naught spent vainly:
Unto Him this little one I render.
Hide the face – the tiny coffin cover:
So, our first dream, our first hope – is over.

The New Year

Who comes dancing over the snow,
His soft little feet all bare and rosy?
Open the door, though the wild winds blow,
Take the child in and make him cosy.
Take him in and hold him dear
He is the wonderful glad New Year.

A Silly Song

'O heart, my heart!' she said, and heard
His mate the blackbird calling,
While through the sheen of the garden green
May rain was softly falling, –
Aye softly, softly falling.

The buttercups across the field
Made sunshine rifts of splendor:
The round snow-bud of the thorn in the wood
Peeped through its leafage tender,
As the rain come softly falling.

'O heart, my heart!' she said and smiled,
'There's not a tree of the valley,
Or a leaf I wis which the rain's soft kiss
Freshens in yonder alley,
Where the drops keep ever falling, –

'There's not a foolish flower i' the grass,
Or bird through the woodland calling,
So glad again of the coming of rain
As I of these tears now falling, –
These happy tears down falling.'

The Young Governess

I mean to be a governess
And earn my daily bread;
For we have many mouths to feed,
And oh! they must be fed –
Anne, Emily, Will, Tom and I,
And little baby Ned.

And though I am but just fourteen,
I'm stout and big and tall,
And I can learn my lessons best,
They say, among us all.
Strong girls like me must never thrust
The weak ones to the wall.

So I'm to be a governess,
And do my busy part
Outside, while others work at home;
Down tears! they must not start!
Who'd tell the children mother died –
Died of a broken heart?

My heart it will not break, I think,
  For I am young and bold;
Much bolder than our Emily,
  Though she's eighteen years old:
I bore all father's angry words
  And looks unkind and cold.

He's gone; and none will hurt us now,
  Young birds in lonely nest,
Trying to keep each other warm,
  Without a mother's breast;
But Tom and I, we're nearly fledged,
  And we shall help the rest.

I will be such a governess!
  Not cross, as you will see;
I'll make my children love their books,
  Just for the love of me –
And work just for the sake of work,
  To reach the top o' the tree.

I'll teach them how to scorn a dunce,
  An idle dunce, I mean:
Those that will learn and those that won't,
  What difference between?
Why, just a wise man and a fool –
  A beggar and a queen!

So I will be a governess
  And earn my daily bread,
Honest and happy, holding high
  My independent head;
O what a merry house we'd be
  If mother were not dead!

OLIVE CUSTANCE

(1874-1944)

Daughter of Colonel Frederic H. Custance, Grenadier Guards, of Weston Old Hall, Norfolk. When she was sixteen she fell in love with the young poet John Gray, but he was destined to remain unmarried and become a Roman Catholic priest. She was one of several notable women writers associated with the publishing house of John Lane, contributing to the *Yellow Book* and other magazines. In 1902 she became engaged to the Hon. George Montagu but married Lord Alfred Douglas, son of the Marquess of Queensbury, by special licence on 4th March. Their son was born within a year. In 1913 she left her husband, and returned to her father's house at Weston.

The Girl in the Glass

Girl in the glass! you smile, and yet
  Your eyes are full of a vague regret;
For dreams are lovely, and life is sad,
And when you were a child what dreams you had!
Now, over your soul life's shadows pass,
    Girl in the glass.

Girl in the glass, an April day
  Looks not more tearful, looks not more gay
Than your rose-flushed face with the wistful mouth.
For your soul seeks Love as a swallow flies south,
So, into your eyes Love's sorrows pass,
  Girl in the glass.

A Lament for the Leaves

The trees look sad – sad – I long for the leaves,
Green leaves that shimmer – and shelter the nests that the song-birds
    make.
The earth is glad – glad – but my spirit grieves.
Break forth from your buds and awake
                O! leaves!

I remember the woods last year and the thick fresh leaves
How they fluttered and flickered and sighed, rustled and quivered
all day...
I almost fancy I hear their song to the breeze,
The fickle breeze that faltered and wavered, but would not stay.
I long for the leaves!

I remember the sun-laced grass, where their shadows were flung
In a tangled web as they trembled – trembled a-tilt on the bough.
Now! they are fallen, alas! from the trees where they hung,
Withered, wind-wafted away... O! where are they now,
The leaves?

The Masquerade

Masked dancers in the Dance of life,
We move sedately... wearily together,
Afraid to show a sign of inward strife,
We hold our souls in tether.

We dance with proud and smiling lips,
With frank appealing eyes, with shy hands clinging.
We sing, and few will question if there slips
A sob into our singing.

Each has a certain step to learn;
Our prisoned feet move staidly in set paces,
And to and fro we pass, since life is stern,
Patiently, with masked faces.

Yet some there are who will not dance,
They sit apart most sorrowful and splendid;
But all the rest trip on as in a trance,
Until the dance is ended.

SARAH DOUDNEY

(1843-1926)

Born in Portsmouth, the youngest child of G.E. Doudney who owned soap works in Portsmouth and Plymouth. Her early childhood was spent in the village of Lovedean, Hampshire. She was educated at Mrs Kendall's school at Southsea, and began to write when very young, soon having her work accepted by several magazines. Her many novels, some written for girls, had a considerable vogue in their day, and her simple prose and verse were said to have been enjoyed by Queen Victoria. She died at Oxford.

The Last Snow of Winter

Soft snow still rests within this wayside cleft,
   Veiling the primrose buds not yet unfurled:
Last trace of dreary winter, idly left
   On beds of moss, and sere leaves crisply curled;
Why does it linger while the violets blow,
                  And sweet things grow?

A relic of long nights and weary days,
   When all fair things were hidden from my sight;
A chill reminder of those mournful ways
   I traversed when the fields were cold and white;
My life was dim, my hopes lay still and low
                  Beneath the snow.

Now spring is coming, and my buried love
   Breaks fresh and strong and living through the sod;
The lark sings loudly in the blue above,
   The budding earth shall magnify her God;
Let the old sorrows and old errors go
                  With the last snow!

HELEN SELINA DUFFERIN, Lady Dufferin
(1806-67)

Eldest of the three beautiful daughters of Thomas Sheridan, colonial treasurer of the Cape of Good Hope, and younger brother of Richard Brinsley Sheridan. One of her sisters was Caroline Norton. She was taken to the Cape of Good Hope by her parents but brought back to England on her father's death in 1817. The rest of her girlhood was spent at Hampton Court Palace in a 'grace and favour' apartment. In 1825 she married Commander Price Blackwood, heir to the Irish title and estate of Baron Dufferin and Clandeboye, and in 1826 became mother of the first Marquess of Dufferin. Her husband died in 1841 and she dedicated herself to supervising her son's education until he came of age. In 1862 she married George Hay, Earl of Gifford, on his death-bed. She is best known as a song-writer but her play *Finesse* was first performed at the Haymarket Theatre in 1863.

from *Meditations on the Poor Law*

An Election Squib

Why should I support my neighbour
On my goods – against my will?
Can't he live by honest labour?
Can't he beg – or can't he steal?
Poor Rates make such sad confusion!
I, for my part, cannot see
How 'John Thomson's' destitution
Gives him any claim on *me*.
'Smith' mayn't own a single penny –
Must I then *my* pound resign?
House and lands – 'Brown' hasn't any,
'Tis no ground for taxing *mine*.
In the present social system
There must still be Poor and Rich;
Some *must* starve (may Heaven assist 'em) –
Then the only question's – which?
I would rather 'twere my neighbour, –
Not from any spite to him!
But the fact is – honest labour
Does not chance to suit my whim:
Stealing – too, is so immoral!
Begging's – a disgusting trade!

(I should feel disposed to quarrel
With a *Saint* – who begs his bread!)
From these facts – my own deduction
Is – that things are well enough:
That the Poor *should* live by suction
And the Rich *should* quaff and stuff.
. . .
Round the Workhouse! round the Poorhouse!
Round the altar! 'round my hat!'
Round the Queen! who (folks assure us)
Only can be saved by that!
And above all, – *round our purses!*
(You round yours – and I – round mine),
Here's – a fig for poor men's curses
Whilst we keep these rules divine.

The Mother's Lament

Showing how a family resemblance is not always desirable

1

It is now nearly forty years, I guess,
Since I was a girl coming out,
And Spriggins proposed – and I said, yes,
At old Lady Mumble's rout.
My match was reckon'd by no means bad,
Take the marrying world as it goes –
But then I must own – Mr. Spriggins had
A remarkably ugly nose!

2

Now the length or shape of your husband's nose
Is a thing that don't signify –
As long as your mother and aunts suppose
There's enough to lead him by!
But I own it often has made me sigh,
At the time of our honeymoon's close –
To hear the folks who were passing by
Remark on my Spriggins's nose!

3

It wasn't round – nor was it square –
Nor three-corner'd as some noses be!
But upon my conscience I do declare
'Twas a mixture of all the three!
And oh! how painful it was to hear,
When our son was in swaddling clothes,
The nurses exclaim – 'Oh, sweet little dear,
He has got his papa's own nose!'

4

Five daughters beside were born to me
To add to my woe and care –
Bell, Susan, Jemima, and Dorothee,
And Kate – who has sandy hair;
But it isn't the number that makes me grieve,
Tho' they cost me a mint in clothes,
– Five gawky girls! – but you'd hardly believe –
They have all got their father's nose!

5

They've been to Brighton for many years past,
And a season in London too,
And Bell nearly got a proposal at last –
But we found that it wouldn't do!
And oh! 'tis a grievous thing, I declare,
To be told, wherever one goes,
'I should know the Miss Sprigginses – anywhere –
They've all got the family nose!'

6

No beau will be seen in our company,
Do all that we possibly can,
Except Mr. Green – who is fifty-three –
And Gubbins – the Doctor's young man!
There's Captain Hodson and Admiral Bluff,
I wonder they don't propose –
For really the girls are well enough –
If they hadn't their father's nose!

To My Dear Son

On his 21st Birthday, with a Silver Lamp, 'Fiat Lux.'

How shall I bless thee? Human love
  Is all too poor in passionate words;
The heart aches with a sense above
  All language that the lip affords:
Therefore a symbol shall express
  My love, – a thing not rare or strange,
But yet – eternal – measureless –
  Knowing no shadow and no change.
Light! which of all the lovely shows
  To our poor world of shadows given,
The fervent Prophet-voices chose
  Alone, as attribute of heaven!

At a most solemn pause we stand,
  From this day forth, for evermore,
The weak but loving human hand
  Must cease to guide thee as of yore.
Then, as thro' life thy footsteps stray,
  And earthly beacons dimly shine,
'Let there be light' upon thy way,
  And holier guidance far than mine!
'Let there be light' in thy clear soul,
  When passion tempts and doubts assail;
When grief's dark tempests o'er thee roll,
  'Let there be light' that shall not fail!

So, Angel-guarded, may'st thou tread
  The narrow path which few may find,
And at the end look back, nor dread
  To count the vanished years behind!
And pray that she, whose hand doth trace
  This heart-warm prayer, – when life is past –
May see and know thy blessed face,
  In God's own glorious light at last!

GEORGE ELIOT, pseudonym of Mary Ann Evans
(1819-80)

Born at Arbury Farm, near Nuneaton, Warwickshire, youngest daughter of Robert Evans, a land agent. Soon after her birth the family moved to Griff, a house on the Arbury estate, where she spent the first twenty-one years of her life. She was educated at schools in Attleboro, Nuneaton and Coventry, and showed early intellectual powers. After the death of her mother in 1836 she kept house for her father in Coventry. Influenced by the freethinker Charles Bray and his wife Caroline, she renounced the narrow evangelical views of her upbringing, moving in with the Brays after her father's death in 1849. She went to London in 1851 to become assistant editor of the *Westminster Review*. There she met Herbert Spencer and George Henry Lewes, and lived with Lewes from 1854 until his death in 1878. A major novelist, the great popularity of her books made her financially secure. In 1880 she married an old friend, John Cross, but died in December of that year.

From *Brother and Sister*

I cannot choose but think upon the time
When our two lives grew like two buds that kiss
At lightest thrill from the bee's swinging chime,
Because the one so near the other is.

He was the elder and a little man
Of forty inches, bound to show no dread,
And I the girl that puppy-like now ran,
Now lagged behind my brother's larger tread.

I held him wise, and when he talked to me
Of snakes and birds, and which God loved the best,
I thought his knowledge marked the boundary
Where men grew blind, though angels knew the rest.

If he said 'Hush!' I tried to hold my breath
Wherever he said 'Come!' I stepped in faith.

Long years have left their writing on my brow,
But yet the freshness and the dew-fed beam
Of those young mornings are about me now,
When we two wandered toward the far-off stream

With rod and line. Our basket held a store
Baked for us only, and I thought with joy
That I should have my share, though he had more,
Because he was the elder and a boy.

The firmaments of daisies since to me
Have had those mornings in their opening eyes,
The bunchèd cowslip's pale transparency
Carries that sunshine of sweet memories,

And wild-rose branches take their finest scent
From those blest hours of infantine content.

...

His sorrow was my sorrow, and his joy
Sent little leaps and laughs through all my frame;
My doll seemed lifeless and no girlish toy
Had any reason when my brother came.

I knelt with him at marbles, marked his fling
Cut the ringed stem and make the apple drop,
Or watched him winding close the spiral string
That looped the orbits of the humming top.

Grasped by such fellowship my vagrant thought
Ceased with dream-fruit dream-wishes to fulfil;
My aëry-picturing fantasy was taught
Subjection to the harder, truer skill

That seeks with deeds so grave a thought-tracked line,
And by 'What is,' 'What will be' to define.

School parted us; we never found again
That childish world where our two spirits mingled
Like scents from varying roses that remain
One sweetness, nor can evermore be singled.

Yet the twin habit of that early time
Lingered for long about the heart and tongue:
We had been natives of one happy clime,
And its dear accent to our utterance clung.

Till the dire years whose awful name is Change
Had grasped our souls still yearning in divorce,
And pitiless shaped them in two forms that range
Two elements which sever their life's course.

But were another childhood-world my share,
I would be born a little sister there.

Roses

You love the Roses – so do I. I wish
The sky would rain down Roses, as they rain
From off the shaken bush. Why will it not?
Then all the valley would be pink and white
And soft to tread on. They would fall as light
As feathers, smelling sweet; and it would be
Like sleeping and like waking, all at once!

ANNE ELLISON

(1823?-   )

Born in Kettering, Northamptonshire. She married and lived for a time in Clough Road, Sheffield, Yorkshire, where her son John was born. After the death of her husband she moved to Ashton-under-Lyne, Lancashire, becoming the schoolmistress at Ashton Workhouse.

An Essay on the Choice of a Husband

Addressed to my tutor

A man to suit me
Must be loving and kind;
With a generous heart,
An intelligent mind;
Honest and sober –
No spendthrift, nor mean,
But moving in that sphere
Which I call between.

His countenance cheerful,
Clever in trade;
Not a coward, nor little,
But tall, and well made.
His age twenty-three;
With dark eyes and hair;
Not effeminate, nor childish –
For that I can't bear.

He must look straight before him.
As though he could see –
For I'll not have a man
Who is squinting at me.
He too must know how
To read, write, and spell;
And be civil to all,
Then he's sure to do well.

Not passionate, mind,
But forgiving and free;
With a heart undivided
And constant to me:
With regular features –
Not too large, or flat;
Though if he was pious,
I should not mind that.

If I get such a husband,
I shall be glad;
I must mind how I choose though –
Some men are so bad.
But this I can say,
Without feeling afraid,
If I see none to suit me,
I'll die an old maid.

I've told you my choice,
So now I'll be neuter;
What there is to correct
I have left to my tutor.

MICHAEL FIELD

Joint pseudonym of Katherine Bradley (1848-1914) and Edith Cooper (1862-1913). Katherine Bradley was the daughter of a Birmingham tobacco manufacturer. She was educated privately and at Newnham College, Cambridge, and the Collège de France, Paris. Her niece, Edith Cooper, was the daughter of her elder sister Emma, wife of J.R. Cooper, a Kenilworth merchant. When Edith's mother became a permanent invalid Katherine joined the Cooper household to help look after the children. Thereafter the aunt and niece lived together as devoted companions, successively in Bristol, Reigate and Richmond, Surrey, the elder educating the younger, and both financially independent. While at Bristol they studied philosophy and the classics at University College. In collaboration they wrote twenty-seven tragedies and eight volumes of verse, operating in such close affinity that their work appeared to be that of a single author. Their small circle of friends included Robert Browning, George Meredith, Herbert Spencer, Oscar Wilde, and George Moore. They became Roman Catholics in 1907, and died of cancer within a year of each other.

Fifty Quatrains

'Twas fifty quatrains: and from unknown strands
The woman came who sang them on the floor.
I saw her, I was leaning by the door,
– Saw her strange raiment and her lovely hands;
And saw . . . but that I think she sang – the bands
Of low-voiced women on a happy shore:
Incomparable was the haze, and bore
The many blossoms of soft orchard lands.
'Twas fifty quatrains, for I caught the measure;
And all the royal house was full of kings,
Who listened and beheld her and were dumb;
Nor dared to seize the marvellous rich pleasure,
Too fearful even to ask in whisperings,
The ramparts being closed, whence she had come.

A Flaw

To give me its bright plumes they shot a jay:
On the fresh jewels, blood! Oh, sharp remorse!
The glittering symbols of the little corse
I buried where the wood was noisome, blind,
Praying that I might nevermore betray
The universe, so whole within my mind.

Nest in Elms

The rooks are cawing up and down the trees!
Ripe as old music is the summer's measure
Of love, of all the busy-ness of leisure,
With dream on dream of never-thwarted ease!
O homely birds, whose cry is harbinger
Of nothing sad, who know not anything
Of sea-birds' loneliness, of Procne's strife,
Rock round me when I die! So sweet it were
To lie by open doors, with you on wing
Humming the deep security of life.

Noon

Full summer and at noon; from a waste bed
Convolvulus, musk-mallow, poppies spread
The triumph of the sunshine overhead.

Blue on refulgent ash-trees lies the heat;
It tingles on the hedge-rows; the young wheat
Sleeps, warm in golden verdure, at my feet.

The pale, sweet grasses of the hayfield blink;
The heath-moors, as the bees of honey drink,
Suck the deep bosom of the day. To think

Of all that beauty by the light defined
None shares my vision! Sharply on my mind
Presses the sorrow: fern and flower are blind.

Song

    A gray mob-cap and a girl's
    Soft circle of sprouting curls,
That proclaim she has had the fever:
How dear the days when the child was nursd!
My God, I pray she may die the first,
    That I may not leave her!
Her head on my knee laid down,
That *duvet* so warm, so brown,
I fondle, I dote on its springing.
'Thou must never grow lonesome or old,
Leave me rather to darkness and cold,
    O my Life, my Singing!'

ELLEN THORNEYCROFT FOWLER

(1860-1929)

Born in Wolverhampton, Staffordshire, the daughter of Henry Hartley Fowler, who became the 1st Viscount Wolverhampton. She wrote verse from the age of seven, and was educated at Fox How School. Her stories were first published in magazines but she progressed to become a popular novelist, some of her novels selling more than 25,000 copies. She had a vivacious personality and was known as a brilliant talker, her conversation sparkling with wit. In 1903 she married A.L. Felkin, an inspector of schools.

The Fiction of To-day

It chanced upon an evil day
  I took a volume in my hand –
A volume which I longed to say
  My soul could understand.

I dipped into its mystic lore
  With all the eagerness of youth,
Nor dreamed but that its pages bore
  The sign and seal of truth.

I viewed it not with such disgust
  As wiser heads would feel for it,
But trusted it as I would trust
  The words of Holy Writ;

Yet when upon its strength I leaned,
  And strove thereby my steps to trace,
It proved as false as any fiend
  And mocked me to my face.

When knowledge to account was turned,
  Who then so great a fool as I?
The so-called science I had learned
  Was one pernicious lie.

Too late it was myself to save
  From mischief which was bound to be;
But woe to whosoever gave
  So base a book to me!

And woe to careless souls and blind
   Who let such trash their tables spread
And leave some fresh, untutored mind
   To read what I have read!

The volume which so grossly lied –
   Which led me wrong and cost me dear –
Was only Bradshaw's Railway Guide
   From some preceding year.

The Great Unfed

A gross neglect doth England's honour stain:
   The Magistrates who wield the legal truncheon,
Who justice execute and truth maintain,
            Receive no luncheon.

The Bench, alas! doth not include the Board.
   If Justice feed not those who wait upon her,
The title of J.P. will be abhorred
            As empty honour.

Stung past endurance by this shame of shames,
   Starved in the absence of sustaining diet,
The inner man indignantly exclaims,
            'Justitia fiat!'

We are aware that Justice cannot see;
   But that she cannot eat it doesn't follow:
She may be blind, but wherefore need she be
            Completely hollow?

They do not wish their noble toil to cease,
   They do not dream of 'dolce far niente,'
These persecuted Justices of Peace
            (But not of plenty):

Envying both the satiated rich
   And the poor man whose mid-day meal a crust is,
'Give us, we pray', they cry, 'something to which
            We may do justice!'

MARY CLARISSA GILLINGTON
(1861-1917)

Born in Audlem, Cheshire, daughter of Rev. John M. Gillington. She was a prolific writer of stories for children, including infants. Her poetry was published in 1892 with that of her sister, Alice Elizabeth Gillington. She married George F. Byron and settled in London, writing as May Byron.

A Dead March

Be hushed, all voices and untimely laughter;
  Let no least word be lightly said
  In the awful presence of the Dead,
    That slowly, slowly this way comes –
Arms piled on coffin, comrades marching after,
    Colours reversed, and muffled drums.

Be bared, all heads; feet, the procession follow
  Throughout the stilled and sorrowing town;
  Weep, woeful eyes, and be cast down;
    Tread softly, till the bearers stop
Under the cypress in the shadowy hollow,
    While last light fades o'er mountain top.

Lay down your burden here, whose life hath journeyed
  Afar, and where ye may not wot;
  Some little while around this spot
    Be dirges sung, and prayers low said,
Dead leaves disturbed, and clammy earth upturnëd;
    Then in his grave dead Love is laid.

Fling them upon him – withered aspirations,
  And battered hopes, and broken vows;
  He was the last of all his house,
    Hath left behind no kith nor kin;
His blood-stained arms and faded decorations,
    His dinted helmet, – throw them in.

And all the time the twilight skies are turning
  To sullen ash and leaden grey;
  Cast the sods o'er him, come away;
    In vain upon his name you call, –
Though you all night should call with bitter yearning,
    He would not heed nor hear at all.

Pass homeward now, in musing melancholy,
  To find the house enfilled with gloom,
  And no lights lit in any room,
    And stinging herald drops of rain;
Choke up your empty heart with anguish wholly,
    For Love will never rise again.

EVA GORE-BOOTH
(1870-1926)

Born at Lissadell, Sligo, third child of Sir Henry Gore-Booth. A delicate child, she was educated privately. From 1897 she lived in Manchester, becoming involved in the women's suffrage movement, and helping to form the Women Textile Workers Union. For a time she served on the Manchester Education Committee and took part in University Settlement activities. The climate affected her health adversely, and after an illness in 1913 she had to move south. Her last years were spent in Hampstead, saddened by the outcome of the 1916 Easter Rebellion, in which her sister Constance, Countess Markiewicz, was implicated. Her poetry shows the influence of Irish legend and scenery, and contains a strong vein of mysticism. Many of her poems were set to music by her friend Max Mayer, the composer.

The Desolate Army

In the world's wars we have no lot nor part,
No tattered flag, no sound of trampling feet
Thrills the dark caverns of a nation's heart
For us, no battle song makes danger sweet.

In the world's praise and love we have no place,
We have not turned the drunkard from his wine –
Nor toiled to build fine dwellings for the race –
Nor burnt new incense at an ancient shrine.

Yet have we seen a glimpse of radiant forms
Behind the blackness of these smoke-stained hours,
Where wisdom shines beyond all clouds and storms,
And pity dwells amongst the steadfast powers.

Then divine madness fills the heart and brain
Of the pale army passionately proud –
We toil on dimly through much strife and strain
To unveil those radiant brows unto the crowd.

Finis

The dogwood's dead, and a mantle red
Over the copse is flung,
Bow down, oh willow, your silver head,
Summer's silver and winter's red
Glory and grey and green have fled,
All winds are silent, all sorrows said,
And all songs sung.

Survival

In the darkness I planted a rose
And it withered and died,
Now a poisonous fungus lives and grows
By the dead rose's side.

Full many an ill weed evil and old
In caves and dungeons thrives,
'Mid poisonous forces manifold
The bitterest life survives.

Out in the fields there's rain and sun
And a rustle of wind-blown wheat,
There's nought to shrink from and nought to shun,
The fittest is honey-sweet.

Honey-sweet from the heart of toil
The inner life of flowers,
The scorching sun and the rain-drenched soil,
The war of living powers.

There is nothing good, there is nothing fair,
Grows in the darkness thick and blind –
Pull down your high walls everywhere,
Let in the sun, let in the wind.

Time

The soul would know the rhythm and sound of time
As men know music, cunning to divide
Into dull bars a melody sublime,
Breaking the song's wings, crushing down her pride.

They follow her swift steps among the flowers,
Thus do we break the radiance of the whole,
Into this rainbow prism of days and hours,
Splitting the absolute glory of the soul.

Then like a milky way of many stars,
The manifold pale fires are brought to birth,
And men grope blindly against iron bars,
And pain and disappointment walk the earth.

The Weaver

I was the child that passed long hours away
Chopping red beetroot in the hay-piled barn;
Now must I spend the wind-blown April day
Minding great looms and tying knots in yarn.

Once long ago I tramped through rain and slush
In brown waves breaking up the stubborn soil,
I wove and wove the twilight's purple hush
To fold about the furrowed heart of toil.

Strange fires and frosts burnt out the seasons' dross,
I watched slow Powers the woven cloth reveal,
While God stood counting out His gain and loss,
And Day and Night pushed on the heavy wheel.

Held close against the breast of living Powers
A little pulse, yet near the heart of strife,
I followed the slow plough for hours and hours
Minding through sun and shower the loom of life.

The big winds, harsh and clear and strong and salt,
Blew through my soul and all the world rang true,
In all things born I knew no stain or fault,
My heart was soft to every flower that grew.

The cabbages in my small garden patch
Were rooted in the earth's heart; wings unseen
Throbbed in the silence under the dark thatch,
And brave birds sang long ere the boughs were green.

Once did I labour at the living stuff
That holds the fire, the water and the wind;
Now do I weave the garments coarse and rough
That some vain men have made for vain mankind.

DORA GREENWELL

(1821-82)

Born at Greenwell Ford, near Lanchester, County Durham, the daughter of a country gentleman and magistrate who became impoverished. Her brother was William Greenwell, the archaeologist. The family home was sold in 1848, when she and her mother went to live in Durham City. After her mother's death she lived mainly in London. A prose-writer, hymn-writer and poet, she also wrote essays on social and medical topics. In 1862 she contributed an article to the *North British Review* in which she earnestly pleaded for the extension of educated women's work. Much of her writing is characterized by deep religious feeling, intensified by poor health, poverty, and lack of a settled home for many years.

Desdichado

Weep not for them who weep
For friend or lover taken hence, for child
That falls 'mid early flowers and grass asleep,
Untempted, undefiled.

Mourn not for them that mourn
For sin's keen arrow with its rankling smart,
God's hand will bind again what He hath torn,
He heals the broken heart.

But weep for him whose eye
Sees in the midnight skies a starry dome
Thick sown with worlds that whirl and hurry by,
And give the heart no home.

Who hears amid the dense
Loud trampling crash and outcry of this wild
Thick jungle world of drear magnificence
No voice which says, *my child*:

Who marks through earth and space
A strange dumb pageant pass before a vacant shrine,
And feels within his inmost soul a place
Unfilled by the Divine.

Weep, weep, for him, above
That looks for God, and sees unpitying Fate,
That finds within his heart, in place of love,
A dull, unsleeping hate.

When the Night and Morning Meet

In the dark and narrow street,
Into a world of woe,
Where the tread of many feet
Went trampling to and fro,
A child was born – speak low!
When the night and morning meet.

Full seventy summers back
Was this, so long ago,
The feet that wore the track
Are lying straight and low;
Yet hath there been no lack
Of passers to and fro

Within the narrow street
This childhood ever played;
Beyond the narrow street
This manhood never strayed;
This age sat still and prayed
Anear the trampling feet.

The tread of ceaseless feet
Flowed through his life, unstirred
By waters' fall, or fleet
Wind music, or the bird
Of morn; these sounds are sweet,
But they were still unheard.

Within the narrow street
  I stood beside a bed,
  I held a dying head
When the night and morning meet;
And every word was sweet,
  Though few the words we said.

And as we talked, dawn drew
  To day, the world was fair
In fields afar, I knew;
  Yet spoke not to him there
Of how the grasses grew,
  Besprent with dewdrops rare.

We spoke not of the sun,
  Nor of this green earth fair;
This soul, whose day was done,
  Had never claimed its share
  In these, and yet its rare
Rich heritage had won.

From the dark and narrow street.
  Into a world of love
A child was born, – speak low,
Speak reverent, for we know
  Not how they speak above,
When the night and morning meet.

LOUISE IMOGEN GUINEY

(1861-1920)

An American living in England. Born in Roxbury, a suburb of Boston, Massachusetts. Her father, a lawyer, was a native of Tipperary. She was educated at the Convent of the Sacred Heart at Elmhurst, Rhode Island. For a time she earned a living as a journalist then became postmistress at Auburndale, Massachusetts. The Protestant community there refused to buy stamps from a Catholic but she received orders from sympathizers all over the United States. After a period working in the Boston Public Library she came to England in 1895, realizing her ambition to study at the Bodleian Library, Oxford. Suffering from deafness and weak eyesight, she was a woman of great charm, and had a devotion to the Cotswold countryside. She died at her home in Chipping Camden, Gloucestershire, and is buried at Wolvercote, near Oxford.

Carol

Vines branching stilly
   Shade the open door
In the house of Sion's lily
   Cleanly and poor.
O, brighter than wild laurel
   The Babe bounds in her hand!
The King, who for apparel
   Hath but a swaddling band,
Who sees her heavenlier smiling than
   Stars in his command.

Soon mystic changes
   Part Him from her breast:
Yet there awhile He ranges
   Gardens of rest,
Yea, she the first to ponder
   Our ransom and recall,
Awhile may rock Him under
   Her young curls' fall,
Against that only tender
   Love loyal heart of all!

What shall inure Him
  Unto the deadly dream
When the tetrarch shall abjure Him,
  The thief blaspheme?
And Scribe and Soldier jostle
  About the shameful Tree,
When even the Apostle
  Demands to touch and see?
But she hath kiss'd her Flower
  Where the wounds are to be.

Strikers in Hyde Park

A woof reversed the fatal shuttles weave,
How slow! but never once they slip the thread.
Hither, upon the Georgian idlers' tread,
Up spacious ways the lindens interleave,
Clouding the royal air since yester-eve,
Come men bereft of time, and scant of bread,
Loud, who were dumb, immortal who were dead,
Through the cowed world their kingdom to retrieve.
What ails thee, England? Altar, mart, and grange
Dream of the knife by night; not so, not so,
The clear Republic waits the general throe,
Along her noonday mountains' open range.
God be with both! for one is young to know
Her mother's rote of evil and of change.

JANET HAMILTON
(1795-1873)

Born in Carshill, Lanarkshire, the daughter of a shoemaker named Thomson. In her childhood the family moved to Hamilton, then to Langloan. For a time her parents became farm labourers, while Janet remained at home, working at the tambour-frame. Eventually her father set up his own shoemaking business, and in 1809 she married John Hamilton, one of his young workmen. They lived together at Langloan for about sixty years and had ten children. She never travelled more than twenty miles from her birthplace, and she became blind eighteen years before her death. In these circumstances her literary output was remarkable, securing a permanent place for her in Scottish literature. She was sometimes known as 'The Coatbridge Poetess'.

From *The Sunday Rail*

(On the first running of Sunday trains on the North British Railway 3 September 1865)

Now range up the carriages, feed up the fires!
To the rail, to the rail, now the pent-up desires
Of the pale toiling million find gracious reply,
On the pinions of steam they shall fly, they shall fly,
The beauties of nature and art to explore,
To ramble the woodlands and roam by the shore.
The city spark here with his smart smirking lass,
All peg-topped and crinolined, squat on the grass,
While with quips and with cranks and soft-wreathed smiles,
Each nymph with her swain the dull Sabbath beguiles.
Here mater and pater familias will come
With their rollicking brood from their close city home.
How they scramble and scream, how they scamper and run,
While pa and mamma are enjoying the fun!
And the urchins bawl out, 'Oh, how funny and jolly,
Dear ma, it is thus to keep Sabbath-day holy.'
Now for pipe and cigar and the snug pocket-flask,
What's the rail on a Sunday without them, we ask?
What the sweet-scented heather and rich clover blooms
To the breath of the weed as it smoulders and fumes?
So in courting and sporting, in drinking and smoking,

Walking and talking, in laughter and joking,
They while the dull hours of the Sabbath away.
What a Sabbath it is! Who is Lord of the day?
Son of man, Son of God, in the sacred record,
'Tis written that Thou art of Sabbath the Lord;
But impious man hath reversed the decree,
And declares himself lord of the Sabbath to be.

ANN HAWKSHAW
(1813-85)

Born at Green Hammerton, Yorkshire, the daughter of the Rev. James Jackson. In 1835 she married John Hawkshaw, a civil engineer. Soon after their marriage her husband was appointed engineer to the Manchester & Bolton Canal & Railway, and subsequently to the Lancashire & Yorkshire Railway. They lived in the Manchester area for more than twenty years, and some of Ann's earliest verse was published in the *Manchester Guardian*. In 1850 they moved to Grosvenor Gardens, London, when John Hawkshaw became a consulting engineer. His works include the railways at Cannon Street and Charing Cross, and he was knighted in 1873.

The City Child's Complaint

'The trees and the flowers are beautiful,
  The sky is blue and high,
And the small streams make pleasant sounds
  As they run swiftly by.

'But all these things are not for me,
  I live amid dark walls;
And scarcely through these dusty panes
  A single sunbeam falls.

'I never hear the wild-bird's song,
  Or see the graceful deer
Go trooping through the forest glades:
  What can I learn from here?

'They say *God's works* are wonderful,
  In sea, and sky, and land;
I never see them, for *men's works*
  Are here on every hand'.

Oh murmur not, thou little one,
  That *here* thy home must be,
And not amid the pleasant fields,
  Or by the greenwood tree.

There is a voice can speak to thee,
   Amid the works of men;
Speak, with a sound as loud and clear,
   As in the lonely glen.

Do not the works thou seest around,
   Spring from man's thoughtful mind,
And in *that*, is there nought of God,
   For thee, for all, to find?

The earth, with all its varied blooms,
   Will have to pass away;
But man's immortal mind will live
   Through everlasting day.

And without mind these sheltering walls
   Around thee had not been;
These busy engines had not moved,
   Nor whirling wheels been seen!

EMILY HICKEY
(1845-1924)

Born in Ireland, the daughter of the Rev. Canon Hickey, she was educated at her home, Macmine Castle, and in a private school. A Catholic, she wrote many devotional poems, and contributed to English and American magazines. She lived in London, attending lectures at University College. Her *Thoughts for Creedless Women* was published in 1906, and *Our Catholic Heritage and English Literature* in 1910. She was a founder member of the Browning Society.

Song

Beloved, it is morn!
  A redder berry on the thorn,
  A deeper yellow on the corn,
For this good day new-born:
    Pray, Sweet, for me
    That I may be
    Faithful to God and thee.

Beloved, it is day!
  And lovers work, as children play,
  With heart and brain untired alway:
Dear love, look up and pray.
    Pray, Sweet, for me
    That I may be
    Faithful to God and thee.

Beloved, it is night!
  Thy heart and mine are full of light,
  Thy spirit shineth clear and white, –
God keep thee in his sight!
    Pray, Sweet, for me
    That I may be
    Faithful to God and thee.

To a Poet

If song is born of sorrow,
  We grudge you not your pain:
Weep your salt tears to-morrow,
  But sing to us again.

If song is born of laughter,
  Laugh with us, at us, too;
But sing, sing to us after,
  For none can sing like you.

Weeping and laughing, poet,
  In soul and voice grow strong;
For this is life, we know it,
  And life is the source of song.

LAURENCE HOPE

Pseudonym of Adela Florence Nicolson (1865-1904). Born at Stoke Bishop, Gloucestershire, the daughter of Arthur Cory, a colonel in the Indian Army. She attended a private school in Richmond, Surrey, before joining her parents in India. In 1889 she married Colonel Malcolm Hassels Nicolson of the Bengal Army, who was aide-de-camp to Queen Victoria from 1891 to 1894. Using her pseudonym she published, in 1901, *The Garden of Karma*, a volume of passionate lyrics with an oriental setting. Her poems were generally reviewed as the work of a man. Such pieces as 'Pale Hands I Loved Beside the Shalimar' became extremely popular as songs. Colonel Nicolson died in Madras in 1904. Two months later his widow, suffering from grief and acute depression, poisoned herself and died at Dunmore House. She and her husband are buried together in St Mary's Cemetery, Madras.

Twilight

Come to me with the earliest star,
    Thou shalt not be caressed,
For passion and love shall stand afar
    That I may give thee rest.
Tell of thy troubles before we sleep
    Of all thy hopes and fears,
And if the telling should make thee weep
    Then I will drink thy tears.

The shade shall solace thy soul that grieves,
    And I shall shield thine eyes,
With glossy fans of magnolia leaves,
    From starlight in the skies,
While all the cares of the angry hosts
    That stalk thy soul by day
Between the trees, like wandering ghosts,
    Shall softly steal away.

Where shouldst thou slumber, if not with me?
    Thy haven is my breast,
I stretch myself as a couch for thee,
    To lull thy limbs to rest.
But, Oh, I promise, Lover of mine,
    By all the stars above
I will not offer my lips to thine,
    Nor weary thee with love!

NORA HOPPER
(1871-1906)

Daughter of an Irishman, Captain Harman Baillie Hopper of the 31st Bengal Infantry, she was born in Exeter, Devonshire, of a Welsh mother, née Francis. Her father died in her early childhood, and she spent her unmarried life with her mother at Sussex Villas, South Kensington, being educated at Cumberland House, Emperor's Gate. She later lived at 36 Royal Crescent, Notting Hill. In 1901 she married Wilfrid Hugh Chesson, the novelist and critic.

A Song of the Road

All the mills in the world are grinding gold grain,
All hearts in the world like my heart should be fain
For my foot goes in time to a holiday measure
And the bird in my bosom is singing for pleasure.

Tall soldiers in gold stand the plumed ranks of corn,
And the poppies are dancing for joy of the morn:
They're gipsies and vagrants, the home-keepers say,
But my heart is at one with the poppies to-day.

I know not what end to my travel shall be,
Or what fairy Prince rides a-seeking for me –
He may be a Sheogue in graithing of gold,
Or a greybeard who tarries for young maids and old.

Meanwhile I go tramping the merry world over,
With the flower of my heart folded close for my lover:
Folded safely and close till my Prince come and claim
The bud long asleep, and the flower turned a flame.

Meanwhile I go tramping, a masterless maid,
With flowers blowing for me in sunshine and shade,
White poppies, red poppies, sea-poppies of amber,
And a wreath for my head of all wild vines that clamber.

I am one with the wind and the flowers in the corn,
And I and the wind laugh aloud in our scorn
At the bedesmen who quarrel earth's meadow lands over,
While there's roses on bushes and honey in clover.

Vagrants

And first the Night, lost in her wild black hair,
Came crooning down the valleys to Kenmare,
    Crooning an old song lost the raths amid,
        Far fallen from love and grace,
    Since days when first the darkness Oscar hid
        And covered Niam's face:
Night, moving slowly, lost in visions sweet
And all the cabins listening for her feet.

And after her came Dawn,
As swift and wild and shy as any fawn.
A glimmer of grey eyes, and moonlit hair,
        A flutter in the air –
A cry of wakening birds, that hardly may
Believe so near the day:
Her feet went by like shadows; from her track
        You saw the dreams draw back.

Then Day came, woman grown, and gravely sweet,
With steady eyes and undelaying feet:
She had no time for dreams, nor yet for song,
        For all day long
Barefooted, mid the children born of her,
She worked among the fields a harvester.

E. F. BRICKDALE
THE FEMALE VAGRANT

MARY HOWITT
(1799-1888)

Born at Coleford, Gloucestershire, the daughter of Samuel Botham, a prosperous Quaker. She was brought up in Uttoxeter, Staffordshire, was educated at home, and began writing verse at an early age. In 1821 she married the writer William Howitt. They settled in Nottingham, where he kept a chemist's shop, then moved to Esher, Surrey, in 1835. She collaborated with her husband in many literary works but also published successful children's books, taught herself Danish and Swedish, and translated many of Hans Christian Andersen's tales, and the Swedish novels of Frederika Bremer. The Literary Academy of Stockholm awarded her a silver medal. She took an active part in the protest of English women against slavery. In 1879 she was awarded a civil list pension of £100 a year. A Quaker for most of her life, she became a Roman Catholic in 1882. Spending the winter in Rome, she died there of bronchitis in January 1888.

Pauper Orphans

They never knew what 't was to play,
Without control, the long long day,
   In wood and field at will;
They knew no tree, no bird, no bud,
They got no strawberries from the wood,
   No wild thyme from the hill.

They play'd not on a mother's floor;
They toil'd amidst the hum and roar
   Of bobbins and of wheels; –
The air they drew was not the mild
Bounty of Nature, but defiled, –
   And scanty were their meals.

Their lives can know no passing joy,
Dwindled and dwarfed are girl and boy,
   And even in childhood old;
With hollow eye and anxious air,
As if a heavy grasping care
   Their spirits did infold.

Their limbs are swollen, their bodies bent,
And worse, no noble sentiment
  Their darken'd minds pervade;
Feeble and blemish'd by disease,
Nothing their marble hearts can please,
  But doings that degrade.

Oh, hapless heirs of want and woe!
What hope of comfort can they know?
  Them man and law condemn;
They have no guide to lead them right,
Darkness they have not known from light, –
  HEAVEN be a friend to them!

The Unregarded Toils of the Poor

Alas! what secret tears are shed,
  What wounded spirits bleed;
What loving hearts are sundered
  And yet man takes no heed!

He goeth in his daily course,
  Made fat with oil and wine,
And pitieth not the weary souls
  That in his bondage pine, –
That turn for him the mazy wheel,
  That delve for him the mine!
And pitieth not the children small
  In noisy factories dim,
That all day long, lean, pale, and faint,
  Do heavy tasks for him!

To him they are but as the stones
  Beneath his feet that lie:
It entereth not his thoughts that they
  From him claim sympathy:
It entereth not his thoughts that God
  Heareth the sufferer's groan,
That in His righteous eye their life
  Is precious as his own.

JEAN INGELOW

(1820-97)

Born in Boston, Lincolnshire, the eldest child of William Ingelow, a banker. Her mother was Scottish, a member of the Kilgour family of Aberdeenshire. Jean's early life was spent in Lincolnshire but she also lived in Ipswich, Suffolk, before settling in London about 1863. There she became acquainted with Tennyson, Ruskin, Froude, Browning, Christina Rossetti, and with most of the poets, painters and writers of the time. She published novels, and stories for children, but is best known for her poetry, of which more than 200,000 copies were sold in the United States alone. Her powerful ballad 'The High Tide on the Coast of Lincolnshire (1571)' is one of the most anthologized Victorian poems. She died at Kensington and is buried at Brompton Cemetery.

Regret

O that word REGRET!
There have been nights and morns when we have sighed,
'Let us alone, Regret! We are content
To throw thee all our past, so thou wilt sleep
For ay.' But it is patient, and it wakes;
It hath not learned to cry itself to sleep.
But plaineth on the bed that it is hard.

We did amiss when we did wish it gone
And over: sorrows humanise our race;
Tears are the showers that fertilise this world;
And memory of things precious keepeth warm
The heart that once did hold them.
They are poor
That have lost nothing; they are poorer far
Who, losing, have forgotten; they most poor
Of all, who lose and wish they MIGHT forget.
For life is one, and in its warp and woof
There runs a thread of gold that glitters fair,
And sometimes in the pattern shows most sweet
Where there are sombre colours. It is true
That we have wept. But oh! this thread of gold,
We would not have it tarnish; let us turn
Oft and look back upon the wondrous web,
And when it shineth sometimes we shall know
That memory is possession.

I

When I remember something which I had,
  But which is gone, and I must do without,
I sometimes wonder how I can be glad,
  Even in cowslip time when hedges sprout;
It makes me sigh to think on it, – but yet
My days will not be better days, should I forget.

II

When I remember something promised me,
  But which I never had, nor can have now,
Because the promiser we no more see
  In countries that accord with mortal vow;
When I remember this, I mourn, – but yet
My happier days are not the days when I forget.

Remonstrance

Daughters of Eve! your mother did not well:
  She laid the apple in your father's hand,
And we have read, O wonder! what befell –
  The man was not deceived, nor yet could stand;
He chose to lose, for love of her, his throne –
With her could die, but could not live alone.

Daughters of Eve! he did not fall so low,
  Nor fall so far, as that sweet woman fell;
For something better, than as gods to know,
  That husband in that home left off to dwell:
For this, till love be reckoned, less than lore,
Shall man be first and best for evermore.

Daughters of Eve! it was for your dear sake
  The world's first hero died an uncrown'd king;
But God's great pity touched the grand mistake,
  And made his married love a sacred thing:
For yet his nobler sons, if aught be true,
Find the lost Eden in their love to you.

Work

Like coral insects multitudinous
  The minutes are whereof our life is made.
  They build it up as in the deep's blue shade
It grows; it comes to light, and then, and thus
For both there is an end. The populous
  Sea-blossoms close, our minutes that have paid
  Life's debt of work are spent; the work is laid
Before their feet that shall come after us.
We may not stay to watch if it will speed;
  The bard if on some luter's string his song
  Live sweetly yet; the hero if his star
Doth shine. Work is its own best earthly meed,
  Else have we none more than the sea-born throng
  Who wrought these marvellous isles that bloom afar.

ELIZA KEARY

(fl.1857-82)

Born in Bilton Rectory, near Wetherby, Yorkshire, daughter of William Keary, rector of the parish and a native of County Galway. Her mother was the daughter of Hall Plumer of Bilton Hall. In conjunction with her elder sister, the novelist Annie Keary, she wrote *Heroes of Asgard*, tales from Scandinavian mythology. After her sister's death in 1879 her *Memoir of Annie Keary* was published in 1882.

Old Age

Such a wizened creature,
   Sitting alone;
   Every kind of ugliness thrown
Into each feature.

'I wasn't always so,'
   Said the wizened
   One; 'sweet motions unimprisoned
Were mine long ago.'

And again, 'I shall be –
   At least something
   Out of this outside me, shall wing
Itself fair and free.'

FRANCES ANNE (FANNY) KEMBLE

(1809-93)

Actress daughter of the actor Charles Kemble, and a niece of Sarah Siddons. She made her first stage appearance at Covent Garden in 1829 as Juliet to her father's Mercutio, and went on to play many leading roles including Portia, Lady Macbeth, Beatrice and Queen Katherine. In 1833 she visited the United States, met and married a Georgia planter, Pierce Butler, but divorced him in 1848. Resuming her maiden name she gave Shakespearian readings for over twenty years, living in America part of the time. A poet and dramatist, she also wrote volumes of personal reminiscences, often indiscreet. She had a sparkling and boisterous personality and held court to a string of elderly admirers that included Edward Fitzgerald, Sidney Smith, Lord Macaulay and other literary men of the time. She died at Gloucester Place, London, and is buried at Kensal Green.

Faith

Better trust all, and be deceived,
   And weep that trust and that deceiving,
Than doubt one heart that, if believed,
   Had blessed one's life with true believing.

O, in this mocking world too fast
   The doubting fiend o'ertakes our youth!
Better be cheated to the last
   Than lose the blessed hope of truth.

On a Hollow Friendship

A bitter cheat! – and here at length it ends –
And thou and I, who were to one another
More closely knit than brother is to brother,
Shall not be even as two common friends.
Never again in our two hearts may grow
The love whose root was bleeding torn away;
Sadly and darkly shall our spirits go.
Companionless, through life's remaining way.
What though still side by side – yet never more

Each answering other, as they did before;
Lonelier by far, than those who ne'er have known
Dear partnership of love such as we knew,
Unpitied by our fellows, to whose view
A seeming false must o'er our state be thrown –
Thus shall we henceforth walk, together – yet alone.

Sicilian Song

I planted in my heart one seed of love,
Watered with tears and watched with sleepless care,
It grew – and when I looked that it should prove
A gracious tree – and blessed harvests bear,
Blossom nor fruit was there to crown my pain,
Tears, care, and labour, all had been in vain;
And yet I dare not pluck it from my heart,
Lest with the deep-struck root my life depart.

The Tender Passion

There's not a fibre in my trembling frame
  That does not vibrate when thy step draws near;
There's not a pulse that throbs not when I hear
  Thy voice, thy breathing, nay, thy very name.
When thou art with me every sense seems dull,
  And all I am, or know, or feel is thee.
My soul grows faint, my veins run liquid flame,
And my bewildered spirit seems to swim
  In eddying whirls of passion dizzily.
When thou art gone there creeps into my heart
  A cold and bitter consciousness of pain:
The light, the warmth of life, with thee depart,
  And I sit dreaming o'er and o'er again,
Thy greeting clasp, thy parting look and tone;
And suddenly I awake – and am alone.

MAY KENDALL
(1861-   )

Born in Bridlington, Yorkshire, and lived there. In addition to poetry she wrote novels and short stories, and collaborated with B.S. Rowntree in writing *How the Labourer Lives.*

Church Echoes

1. Vicar's Daughter.

Down in the depths of this fair church –
A man may find them if he search,
There lie six pews that are called Free,
And there the strange Bohemians be.
(Have mercy upon them, miserable offenders).

We Philistines in cushioned pews
Have prayer-books more than we can use.
They have one prayer-book that they share.
They do not kneel: they sit and stare.
(Have mercy upon them, miserable offenders).

Decorously we must meet their view
As if they were an empty pew.
We are above them and beyond,
And reverently we respond.
(Have mercy upon them, miserable offenders).

2. Charity Child.

The Vicar's daughters look so good,
We think that they are made of wood.
Like rests for hymn-books, there they stand,
With each a hymn-book in her hand.

Half through the sermon once we tried
To hold our eyelids open wide,
That we might know if they *could* keep
Awake, or sometimes went to sleep.

It was no use, we may be wrong.
The Vicar preached so very long;
And keep awake we never could –
We *think* that they are made of wood.

3. Tramp.

Hardly includes us in its glance
The Vicar's glassy countenance:
The Verger with superior eyes
Surveys us in a still surprise.

But when the organ's notes begin
I need not any Philistine:
To hear the music is my bliss;
And I'm at home where music is.

Through ranks of aliens to and fro
I see the true musician go.
So dim their eyes, they cannot trace
The light unknown upon his face.

Here week by week I come, and see
No hand stretched out to welcome me;
And I am in a friendless land –
But music takes me by the hand.

HARRIET ELEANOR HAMILTON KING

(1840-1920)

Born in Edinburgh, daughter of Admiral W.A. Baillie Hamilton and Lady Harriet Hamilton, sister of the Duke of Abercorn. From her sixth year to the time of her marriage most of her life was spent in London and Blackheath. In 1863 she married Henry S. King, the banker and publisher. She resided at the Manor House, Chigwell, Essex, all her married life, removing to another part of the county after her husband's death. Some of her poems had Italian themes and, although she had not visited Italy, her 'guides' to that country were Murray's handbooks. She had a strong and sympathetic interest in the cause of Italian republicanism, and wrote a biography of Giuseppe Mazzini.

From *Working Girls in London*

Is it not the time of flowers,
    And of birds that sing?
Here we know the days and hours,
    Not the Spring.

Is not this the age for pleasure,
    And for holidays?
We have neither ease nor leisure,
    Work always.

Are not ripe fruits now in season,
    Honey, cream, and cake?
Daily bread for us is reason
    Thanks to make.

Are not these the days for playing
    On the garden-grass?
We, our daily work delaying,
    Starve, alas!

Are not these the nights for wearing
    Robes of gossamer?
Summer finds us burdens bearing,
    Spite of her.

Are not cool streams flowing whitely,
    Water-lily lit?
Here within close walls we nightly
    Stifling sit.

Is not this the month for lying
    In the green leaves' shade?
Summer breezes fresh are flying,
    Fast we fade.

If of good things life bereft us
    What avails the rest?
Still the better things are left us
    And the best.

Are not some among you living
    Who can cheer the way?
Yes, their lives in service giving,
    Day by day.

Would you not with your rich neighbour
    Change, and cast off care?
Christ our poverty and labour
    Chose to share.

ISA CRAIG KNOX

(1831-1903)

Born in Edinburgh, only daughter of a hosier named Craig. Orphaned as a child, she was brought up by her grandmother. She left school at the age of ten, began contributing verse to *The Scotsman* under the pseudonym 'Isa', and eventually joined the editorial staff. In 1857 she moved to London to take up the position of assistant secretary to the Social Science Association, an appointment which proved controversial. A year later she resigned on marriage to her cousin, John Knox, an iron merchant. She continued to campaign for the women's movement, and was a member of the Ladies' Sanitary Association, founded in 1859 to educate on hygiene and health care.

The Root of Love

Unto a goodly tree –
A rose-tree – in the garden of my heart,
Grew up my love for thee!

Truth for its spreading root,
That drew the sweetest virtue of the soil
Up to the freshest shoot.

My tree was richly clad;
All generous thoughts and fancies burst the bud,
And every leaf was glad.

The last of all, the flower,
The perfect flower of love, herself proclaimed
And ruled from hour to hour.

There came a thunder rain,
But for each full-blown bloom it scattered down,
Fresh buds it opened twain.

There came a wind that reft
Both leaf and flower, and broke both branch and stem;
Only the root was left.

The root was left, and so
The living rose lay hidden till the time
When the sweet south should blow.

LUCY KNOX
(1845-84)

Daughter of Stephen E. Spring-Rice. Her grandfather, Thomas Spring-Rice, was the 1st Baron Monteagle of Brandon, in Kerry, and Chancellor of the Exchequer, 1835-39. Her brother succeeded to the title. In 1866 she married Octavius Newry Knox.

Lines

Strong in my youth I stood awaiting joy:
One passed, and, smiling with his eyes at mine,
Knew not his coming and his going turned
My whole bright world into an empty shrine.

Ah! thus the Sun, whose beams delight the world,
Kisses, at unawares, some tender spray,
Which, all unfolding, in a late frost dies,
While the great Sun, rejoicing, goes his way.

Sonnet

I have no wealth of grief; no sobs, no tears,
Not any sighs, no words, no overflow
Nor storms of passion; no reliefs, yet oh!
I have a leaden grief and with it fears
Lest they who think there's nought where nought appears
May say I never loved him. Ah not so!
Love for him fills my heart; if grief is slow
In utterance remember that for years
Love was a habit and the grief is new,
So new a thing it has no language yet.
Tears crowd my heart: with eyes that are not wet
I watch the rain-drops, silent, large and few,
Blotting a stone; then comforted I take
Those drops to be my tears, shed for his sake.

LOUISE DANSE

EMILY LAWLESS
(1845-1913)

Born at Lyons, County Kildare, one of the eight children of the 3rd Baron Cloncurry. Her childhood was spent in the west of Ireland, where she was privately educated by governesses. Apart from some continental travel and occasional visits to Dublin and London, most of her life was spent on the family estate. She wrote novels, poetry, historical studies, a biography of Maria Edgeworth, numerous short stories, and might be regarded as a forerunner of the literary renaissance. Her patriotic verse on Irish historical themes is often found in anthologies but her other poetry is largely unknown. Although her health was not good, she rode to hounds and enjoyed exploring Connemara, the Aran Islands and other wild uninhabited countryside. She had a passion for gardening and was a skilled landscape gardener. After her mother's death she moved to England, setting up home at Hazelhatch, Gomshall, Surrey, with her devoted friend Lady Sarah Spencer.

A Retort

Stud all your shores with prosperous towns!
Blacken your hill-sides, mile on mile!
Redden with bricks your patient downs!
And proudly smile.

A day will come before you guess,
A day when men of clearer sight
Will rue that deed beyond redress
Will loathe the sight.

And, loathing, fly the hateful place,
And, shuddering, quit the hideous thing,
For where unblackened rivers race,
And skylarks sing.

For where, remote from smoke and noise,
Old Leisure sits knee-deep in grass;
Where simple days bring simple joys
And lovers pass.

I see an envied haunt of peace,
Calm and untouched, remote from roar,
Where wearied men may from their burdens cease
On a still shore.

Wishes

I would I were you, you scaly fish,
swim-swimming in the sea,
Or a fox upon the hillside there,
a hunter bold and free,
Anything but the man I am,
crying, dear God, to thee!

I would I were you, you black sea-weed,
toss-tossing on the sea,
Or you, or you, grey humps of stone,
which feel no misery –
I pray you make me as these, dear God,
since better may not be!

AMY LEVY

(1861-89)

Born in Clapham, south-west London, of Jewish parents, Lewis and Isabelle Levy. In 1876 the family moved to Brighton where Amy was educated before going up to Newnham College, Cambridge. *Xantippe*, her first book of verse, was published while she was still at Cambridge. A novelist as well as a poet, her work reflects her own melancholy nature and demonstrates her sensitivity to pain and tragedy. On 10th September 1889 she committed suicide by suffocating herself with charcoal fumes at her parents' house in Endsleigh Gardens, London. The coroner's verdict was 'self-destruction... cause unknown'.

Ballade of an Omnibus

Some men to carriages aspire;
On some the costly hansoms wait;
Some seek a fly, on job or hire;
Some mount the trotting steed, elate.
I envy not the rich and great,
A wandering minstrel, poor and free,
I am contented with my fate –
An omnibus suffices me.

In winter days of rain and mire
I find within a corner strait;
The busmen know me and my lyre
From Brompton to the Bull-and-Gate.
When summer comes, I mount in state
The topmost summit, whence I see
Croesus look up, compassionate –
An omnibus suffices me.

I mark, untroubled by desire,
Lucullus' phaeton and its freight.
The scene whereof I cannot tire,
The human tale of love and hate,
The city pageant, early and late
Unfolds itself, rolls by, to be
A pleasure deep and delicate.
An omnibus suffices me.

Princess, your splendour you require,
I, my simplicity; agree
Neither to rate lower nor higher.
An omnibus suffices me.

Epitaph

(On a commonplace person who died in bed)

This is the end of him, here he lies:
The dust in his throat, the worm in his eyes,
The mould in his mouth, the turf on his breast;
This is the end of him, this is best.
He will never lie on his couch awake,
Wide-eyed, tearless, till dim daybreak.
Never again will he smile and smile
When his heart is breaking all the while.
He will never stretch out his hands in vain
Groping and groping – never again.
Never ask for bread, get a stone instead,
Never pretend that the stone is bread.
Never sway and sway 'twixt the false and true,
Weighing and noting the long hours through.
Never ache and ache with the choked-up sighs;
This is the end of him, here he lies.

Straw in the Street

Straw in the street where I pass to-day
Dulls the sound of the wheels and feet.
'Tis for a failing life they lay
Straw in the street.

Here, where the pulses of London beat,
Someone strives with the Presence grey;
Ah, is it victory or defeat?

The hurrying people go their way,
Pause and jostle and pass and greet;
For life, for death, are they treading, say,
                    Straw in the street?

CAROLINE LINDSAY, Lady Lindsay

(1844-1912)

The only daughter and heir of the Right Hon. Henry Fitz-Roy. In 1864 she married Sir Coutts Lindsay, an army officer who was commandant of the British Italian Legion, and Deputy-Lieutenant of Fifeshire. They lived at 11 Grosvenor Square, London. Lady Lindsay was a novelist, short story writer and poet, and also wrote books for children.

A Cradle Song

Lullaby, lullaby, my little son.
Lullaby, lullaby, my pretty one.

What shall I bring to thee?
What shall I sing for thee?

Unto her roost the sparrow goes,
In sleep the red-tipped daisies close,
The golden lights fade on the hill,
High on the trees the leaves are still.

Lullaby, lullaby, my little son.
Lullaby, lullaby, my pretty one.

What be thy dreams, and canst thou see
Into thine own futurity?
Thy frame is of such tiny span –
Yet may my babe become a man.

Lullaby, lullaby, my little son.
Lullaby, lullaby, my pretty one.

Those rosy cheeks and curled-up feet
Are fair and dear and tender-sweet,
And close I hold my darling boy
That is my love and hope and joy.

Lullaby, lullaby, my little son.
Lullaby, lullaby, my pretty one.

The Saviour was a babe also,
One Christmas-tide, long, long ago;
And now He gazes down on thee,
With love on thee, on thee and me.

  Lullaby, lullaby, my little son.
  Lullaby, lullaby, my pretty one.

    What shall I bring to thee?
    What shall I sing for thee?

December Song

  Who would thy laureate be
   And tune for thee,
O cruel Winter, churlish king,
Grim lord of dearth, and ice, and snow,
That com'st with footstep hard and slow,
Across the brown and withered leaves
To store thy diamonds in our eaves?
  Who would thy triumph sing?

  No heralds thine, as they,
   In bright array,
That weave for Spring her rainbow dress;
Brave maids, they greet her waking hour –
Primrose, Lent lily, and Wind-flower.
What though thy frost mandate's writ
On twinkling lattice-panes – can it
  Command our tenderness?

  Yet given to thee is grace
   Of noblest place
'Mong seasons of our changing earth.
For He who rules each yearly round
Was lowly born on wintry ground.
Yea, Winter brings the Christmas time;
White Winter, ringing Christmas chime,
  Rings in the White Christ's birth.

ROSAMUND MARRIOTT WATSON

(1863-1911)

American-born essayist, poet, and author of one novel, she wrote under the name Graham R. Tomson. She married Henry Brereton Marriott Watson, an Australian journalist and writer settled in London. Latterly they lived at Shere, Surrey.

In a London Garden

O hanging linden leaves the lamp shines through,
Loose-dropping discs of limpid yellow lustre,
Like magic fruits upon the dusky blue;
Voiceless and viewless as the falling dew,
Unshapen dreams amid your shadows cluster.

O dreaming air! your dream must needs be sweet,
The secret thought you fain would tell but dare not.
One with the message of the passing feet,
The roll of wheels, the murmur of the street,
Be it false or true, be it life or death, I care not.

O luminous dusk! Heart of the summer night!
Hold fast your secret, breathe the watchword never.
Keep it inviolate, veiled from sense and sight;
Safe from disclosure's disenchanting blight,
Dear and desired, unknown, beloved for ever.

To My Cat

Half loving-kindliness and half disdain,
   Thou comest to my call serenely suave,
With humming speech and gracious gestures grave,
In salutation courtly and urbane;
Yet must I humble me thy grace to gain,
   For wiles may win thee though no arts enslave,
   And nowhere gladly thou abidest save
Where naught disturbs the concord of thy reign.

Sphinx of my quiet hearth! who deign'st to dwell
  Friend of my toil, companion of mine ease,
  Thine is the lore of Ra and Rameses;
That men forget dost thou remember well,
  Beholden still in blinking reveries
With sombre, sea-green gaze inscrutable.

ANNIE MATHESON

(1853-1924)

Born at Blackheath, London, daughter of the Rev. James Matheson, Congregational minister. Author of a number of children's books, a biography of Florence Nightingale, and introductions to the novels of George Eliot. Some of her work was published by the Oxford University Press, and two of her poems are included in *The Oxford Book of Victorian Verse*, 1912. A note in the *Journal of Education*, 1899, states 'The keynote of her poetry is Christian socialism tempered by mystic optimism'. She lived latterly at Maybury Hill, Woking, Surrey.

A Song of Handicrafts

The Weaver

Sunlight from the sky's own heart,
  Flax unfolded to receive:
Out of sky and flax and art,
  Lovely raiment I achieve –
Earth a part and heaven a part,
  God in all, for Whom I weave!

The Carpenter

Deep into the wood I hew,
  A message fell from the sun's lip;
Fire and strength it downward drew
  For the faggot and the ship:
God's own, in the forest, grew
  Timber that I hew and chip.

The Mason

Out of clay or living rock
  I will make my brick or stone:
At the door of God I knock,
  Builder whose command I own,
Who can birth and death unlock,
  And in dust can find a throne.

Chorus

Mighty Craftsman! craftsmen, we,
  Feel Thy spirit in our hands:
All the worlds are full of Thee –
  Wake our eyes and break our bands –
Servants, and for ever free,
  Sons, and heirs of all thy lands!

ALICE MEYNELL
(1847-1922)

Born at Barnes near London; née Thompson. Her father was a scholar, her mother a concert pianist, and her sister the military painter Elizabeth Butler. Most of her childhood was spent abroad, in Italy, France and Switzerland. A poet and essayist, she was converted to Roman Catholicism in 1869 and carried her religious beliefs into her writing. Her output of prose and verse was always fine in style and content. While she was still a girl her poems had been warmly praised by established writers. In 1877 she married the author and journalist Wilfrid Meynell, by whom she had eight children. In their hospitable home she and her husband were on intimate terms with the great literary figures of the time – Browning, Tennyson, Ruskin, Rossetti, Patmore, Meredith, and George Eliot.

Chimes

Brief, on a flying night
   From the shaken tower,
A flock of bells take flight,
   And go with the hour.

Like birds from the cote to the gales,
   Abrupt – O hark!
A fleet of bells set sails,
   And go to the dark.

Sudden the cold airs swing,
   Alone, aloud,
A verse of bells takes wing
   And flies with the cloud.

From *A Letter from a Girl to Her Own Old Age*

Listen, and when thy hand this paper presses,
O time-worn woman, think of her who blesses
What thy thin fingers touch, with her caresses.

O mother, for the weight of years that break thee!
O daughter, for slow Time must yet awake thee,
And from the changes of my heart must make thee.

O fainting traveller, morn is grey in heaven.
Dost thou remember how the clouds were driven?
And are they calm about the fall of even?

Pause near the ending of thy long migration,
For this one sudden hour of desolation
Appeals to one hour of thy meditation.

Suffer, O silent one, that I remind thee
Of the great hills that stormed the sky behind thee,
Of the wild winds of power that have resigned thee.

Know that the mournful plain where thou must wander
Is but a grey and silent world, but ponder
The misty mountains of the morning yonder.

Listen: – the mountain winds with rain were fretting,
And sudden gleams the mountain-tops besetting.
I cannot let thee fade to death, forgetting.

What part of this wild heart of mine I know not
Will follow with thee where the great winds blow not,
And where the young flowers of the mountain grow not.
. . .
I have not writ this letter of divining
To make a glory of thy silent pining,
A triumph of thy mute and strange declining.

Only one youth, and the bright life is shrouded.
Only one morning, and the day was clouded.
And one old age with all regrets is crowded.

O hush, O hush! Thy tears my words are steeping.
O hush, hush, hush! So full, the fount of weeping?
Poor eyes, so quickly moved, so near to sleeping?

Pardon the girl; such strange desires beset her.
Poor woman, lay aside the mournful letter
That breaks thy heart; the one who wrote, forget her:

The one who now thy faded features guesses,
With filial fingers thy grey hair caresses,
With morning tears thy mournful twilight blesses.

November Blue

The golden tint of the electric lights seems to give a complementary colour to the air in the early evening – Essay on London.

O heavenly colour, London town
  Has blurred it from her skies;
And, hooded in an earthly brown,
  Unheaven'd the city lies.
No longer standard-like this hue
  Above the broad road flies;
Nor does the narrow street the blue
  Wear, slender pennon-wise.

But when the gold and silver lamps
  Colour the London dew,
And, misted by the winter damps,
  The shops shine bright anew –
Blue comes to earth, it walks the street,
  It dyes the wide air through;
A mimic sky about their feet,
  The throng go crowned with blue.

Parted

Farewell to one now silenced quite,
Sent out of hearing, out of sight, –
  My friend of friends, whom I shall miss.
  He is not banished, though, for this, –
Nor he, nor sadness, nor delight.

Though I shall walk with him no more,
A low voice sounds upon the shore.
  He must not watch my resting-place
  But who shall drive a mournful face
From the sad winds about my door?

I shall not hear his voice complain
But who shall stop the patient rain?
  His tears must not disturb my heart,
  But who shall change the years, and part
The world from every thought of pain?

Although my life is left so dim,
The morning crowns the mountain-rim;
  Joy is not gone from summer skies,
  Nor innocence from children's eyes,
And all these things are part of him.

He is not banished, for the showers
Yet wake this green warm earth of ours.
  How can the summer but be sweet?
  I shall not have him at my feet,
And yet my feet are on the flowers.

The Rainy Summer

There's much afoot in heaven and earth this year;
   The winds hunt up the sun, hunt up the moon,
Trouble the dubious dawn, hasten the drear
   Height of a threatening noon.

No breath of boughs, no breath of leaves, of fronds
   May linger or grow warm; the trees are loud;
The forest, rooted, tosses in his bonds,
   And strains against the cloud.

No scents may pause within the garden-fold;
   The rifled flowers are cold as ocean shells;
Bees, humming in the storm, carry their cold
   Wild honey to cold cells.

The Roaring Frost

A flock of wings came flying from the North,
Strong birds with fighting pinions driving forth
      With a resounding call: –

Where will they close their wings and cease their cries –
Between what warming seas and conquering skies –
      And fold, and fall?

A Song of Derivations

I come from nothing; but from where
Come the undying thoughts I bear?
  Down, through long links of death and birth,
  From the past poets of the earth.
My immortality is there.

I am like the blossom of an hour.
But long, long vanished sun and shower
  Awoke my breath i' the young world's air
  I track the past back everywhere
Through seed and flower and seed and flower.

Or I am like a stream that flows
Full of the cold springs that arose
  In morning lands, in distant hills;
  And down the plain my channel fills
With melting of forgotten snows.

Voices, I have not heard, possessed
My own fresh songs; my thoughts are blessed
  With relics of the far unknown.
  And mixed with memories not my own
The sweet streams throng into my breast.

Before this life began to be,
The happy songs that wake in me
  Woke long ago and far apart.
  Heavily on this little heart
Presses this immortality.

ROSA MULHOLLAND
(1841-1921)

Born in Belfast, the daughter of a doctor, she was educated privately at home. A prolific writer for the popular press, and of novels with an Irish setting, her fiction is overly romantic and heavily religious. It was said that she wrote for 'the nobler and purer-minded section of the reading public'. In 1891 she married Sir John T. Gilbert, the historian, and she published a biography of him in 1905. Latterly she lived at Villa Nova, Blackrock, County Dublin.

Lullaby

Lullaby sweet, my baby love,
    For the dew is on the rose;
Mother will rock her treasure, singing,
    Till the drooping eye-lids close.
The slim white angels are winging, winging,
    Down from the silver moon, O
Lullaby sweet, my baby bird,
    While mother will rock and croon.

The wild wood-doves in the oaks above
    Are cooing soft in their dreams,
And the drowsy air a whisper is holding
    With the sleepy mountain streams.
Deep in the pool the lily golden
    Is closing her brilliant eyes, O
Lullaby sweet, my baby dear,
    For the stars flash out in the skies!

Lullaby sweet, my babe of pearl;
    Now close, my lily flower!
The thrush has forgot his music mellow,
    The blackbird's asleep in his bower.
On mother's bosom is made thy pillow,
    Her love sweet watch will keep, O
Rocked in her arms, till sunrise hour
    Sleep softly – sleep, oh! sleep.

EDITH NESBIT

(1858-1924)

Born in London, the daughter of John Collis Nesbit, an agricultural chemist. She was educated at a French convent, spending her early youth in the country at Holstead Hall, Kent. She began her literary career by writing verse but is best remembered by her very successful children's stories. In 1880 she married the socialist writer Hubert Bland. Theirs was an unconventional household – she brought up the two children of her husband and his mistress (her companion and housekeeper) as part of the family alongside her own children. She took a keen interest in socialism, and in 1883 was one of the founders of the 'Fellowship of New Life' out of which sprang the Fabian Society. After Bland's death she married Thomas Tucker, an engineer, and retired to New Romney. She was a woman of striking appearance and great personal charm.

At Parting

And you could leave me now –
After the first remembered whispered vow
Which sings for ever and ever in my ears –
The vow which God among His Angels hears –
After the long-drawn years,
The slow, hard tears,
Could break new ground, and wake
A new strange garden to blossom for your sake,
And leave me here alone,
In the old garden that was once our own?

How should I learn to bear
Our garden's pleasant ways and pleasant air,
Her flowers, her fruits, her lily, her rose and thorn,
When only in the picture these appear –
These, once alive, and always over-dear?
Ah – think again: the rose you used to wear
Must still be more than other roses be
The flower of flowers. Ah, pity, pity me!

For in my acres is no plot of ground
Whereon could any garden site be found:
I have but little skill
To water, weed, and till,

And make the desert blossom like the rose;
Yet our old garden knows
If I have loved its ways and walks and kept
The garden watered, and the pleasance swept.

Yet – if you must – go now:
Go, with my blessing filling both your hands,
And, mid the desert sands
Which life drifts deep round every garden wall
Make your new festival
Of bud and blossom – red rose and green leaf.
No blight born of my grief
Shall touch your garden, love; but my heart's prayer
Shall draw down blessings on you from the air,
And all we learned of leaf and plant and tree
Shall serve you when you walk no more with me
In garden ways; and when with her you tread
The pleasant ways with blossoms overhead,
And when she asks, 'How did you come to know
The secrets of the way these green things grow?'
Then you will answer – and I, please God, hear,
'I had another garden once, my dear.'

Baby's Birthday

G.T.A.

Before your life that is to come,
Love stands with eager eyes, that vainly
  Seek to discern what gift may fit
  The slow unfolding years of it;
And still Time's lips are sealed and dumb,
And still Love sees no future plainly.

We cannot guess what flowers will spring
Best in your garden, bloom most brightly;
  But some fair flowers in any plot
    Will spring and grow, and wither not;
And such wish-flowers we gladly bring,
And in that small hand lay them lightly.

Baby, we wish that those dear eyes
May see fulfilment of our dreaming,
Those little feet may turn from wrong,
Those hands to hold the right be strong,
That heart be pure, that mind be wise
To know the true from the true-seeming.

We wish that all your life may be
A life of selfless brave endeavour –
That for reward the fates allow
Such love as lines your soft nest now
To warm the years for you, when we,
Who wish you this, are cold for ever.

A Great Industrial Centre

Squalid street after squalid street,
Endless rows of them, each the same,
Black dust under your weary feet,
Dust upon every face you meet,
Dust in their hearts, too – or so it seems –
Dust in the place of dreams.

Spring in her beauty thrills and thrives,
Here men hardly have heard her name.
Work is the end and aim of their lives –
Work, work, work! for children and wives;
Work for a life which, when it is won,
Is the saddest under the sun!

Work – one dark and unending round
In black dull workshops, out of the light;
Work that others' ease may abound,
Work that delight for them may be found,
Work without hope, without pause, without peace,
That only in death can cease.

Brothers, who live glad lives in the sun,
  What of these men, at work in the night?
God will ask you what you have done;
Their lives be required of you – every one –
Ye, who were glad and who liked life well,
    While they did your work – in hell!

In the Cabinet Drawer

With the amethyst necklace she carried,
  Laid by with the scraps of her lace;
And the bonnet she wore to be married,
  My young mother's face.

The very same bonnet looms large in
  The photograph's yellowish shade,
With 'Studio' below in the margin,
  'Smith, Brighton Parade'.

There's the smile the photographer ordered,
  The dear little head tilted back;
The dress was a lilac, and bordered
  With patterns in black.

It was crinoline-time, and they trimmed it
  With terrible trimmings of gimp;
How quaint! It's my tears that have dimmed it –
  The border is limp.

She was but a child when she married,
  And younger than I when she died;
And here is the rose that she carried
  When she was a bride.

For the touch of my fingers upon it,
  The print of my tears and my kiss
On the bright little face in the bonnet –
  Time leaves me but this!

CAROLINE NORTON
(1808-77)

Distinguished for her beauty and her wit, she was one of the daughters of Thomas Sheridan and a sister of Lady Dufferin. In 1827 she married the Hon. George Norton, a marriage which ended in conflict and separation. She became a novelist, poet and popular writer in periodicals. Her unhappy marriage and her subsequent legal battle for custody of her three sons contributed to the amelioration of the laws affecting the social conditions of women. In 1877 she married Sir William Stirling Maxwell, her first husband having died in 1875.

Crippled Jane

They said she might recover, if we sent her down
to the sea,
But that is for rich men's children, and we knew it
could not be:
So she lived at home in the Lincolnshire Fens, and
we saw her, day by day,
Grow pale, and stunted, and crooked; till her last
chance died away.
And now *I'm* dying; and often, when you thought
that I moaned with pain,
I was moaning a prayer to Heaven, and thinking of
Crippled Jane.
Folks will be kind to Johnny; his temper is merry
and light;
With so much love in his honest eyes, and a sturdy
sense of right.
And no one could quarrel with Susan; so pious,
and meek, and mild,
And nearly as wise as a woman, for all that she looks
such a child!
But Jane will be weird and wayward; fierce, and
cunning, and hard;
She won't believe she's a burden, be thankful, nor
win regard.
God have mercy upon her! God be her guard and
guide;

How will strangers bear with her, when, at times,
even I felt tried?
When the ugly smile of pleasure goes over her
sallow face,
And the feeling of health, for an hour, quickens her
languid pace;
When with dwarfish strength she rises, and plucks,
with a selfish hand,
The busiest person near her, to lead her out on the
land;
Or when she sits in some corner, no one's
companion or care,
Huddled up in some darksome passage, or crouched
on a step of the stair;
While far off the children are playing, and the birds
singing loud in the sky,
And she looks through the cloud of her headache,
to scowl at the passers-by.
I die – God have pity upon her! – how happy rich
men must be! –
For they said she might have recovered – if we sent
her down to the sea.

I Do Not Love Thee

I do not love thee! – no! I do not love thee!
And yet when thou art absent I am sad;
And envy even the bright blue sky above thee,
Whose quiet stars may see thee and be glad.

I do not love thee! – yet, I know not why,
Whate'er thou dost seems still well done, to me:
And often in my solitude I sigh
That those I do love are not more like thee!

I do not love thee! – yet, when thou art gone,
I hate the sound (though those who speak be dear)
Which breaks the lingering echo of the tone
Thy voice of music leaves upon my ear.

I do not love thee! – yet thy speaking eyes,
With their deep, bright, and most expressive blue,
Between me and the midnight heaven arise,
Oftener than any eyes I ever knew.

I do not love thee! yet, alas!
Others will scarcely trust my candid heart;
And oft I catch them smiling as they pass,
Because they see me gazing where thou art.

Ifs

Oh, if the winds could whisper what they hear,
When murmuring round at sunset through the grove;
If words were written on the streamlet clear,
So often spoken fearlessly above:
If tale-tell stars descending from on high,
Could image forth the thoughts of all that gaze,
Entranced upon that deep cerulean sky,
And count how few think *only* of their rays!

If the lulled heaving ocean could disclose
All that has passed upon her golden sand,
When the moon-lighted waves triumphant rose,
And dashed their spray upon the echoing strand.
If dews could tell how many tears have mixed
With the bright gem-like drops that Nature weeps,
If night could say how many eyes are fixed
On *her* dark shadows, while creation sleeps!

If echo, rising from her magic throne,
Repeated with her melody of voice
Each timid sigh – each whispered word and tone,
Which made the hearer's listening heart rejoice.
If nature could, unchecked, repeat aloud
All she hath heard and seen – must hear and see –
Where would the whispering, vowing, sighing crowd
Of lovers, and their blushing partners, be?

FANNY PARNELL

(1854-82)

Born at Avondale, County Wicklow, into a Cheshire family long settled in Ireland. Her brother was the Irish nationalist and politician Charles Stewart Parnell. When she was only ten years old her verses were published in *The Irish People*. Much involved in Land League agitation and in Irish politics in general, she assisted in organizing the Ladies' Land League, and wrote many poems for the nationalist press. She died in Bordentown, New York.

After Death

Shall mine eyes behold thy glory, O my country?
  Shall mine eyes behold thy glory?
Or shall the darkness close around them, ere the sunblaze
  Break at last upon thy story?

When the nations ope for thee their queenly circle,
  As a sweet new sister hail thee,
Shall these lips be sealed in callous death and silence,
  That have known but to bewail thee?

Shall the ear be deaf that only loved thy praises,
  When all men their tribute bring thee?
Shall the mouth be clay that sang thee in thy squalor,
  When all poets' mouths shall sing thee?

Ah! the harpings and the salvos and the shoutings
  Of thy exiled sons returning!
I should hear, tho' dead and mouldered, and the grave-damps
  Should not chill my bosom's burning.

Ah! the tramp of feet victorious! I should hear them
  'Mid the shamrocks and the mosses,
And my heart should toss within the shroud and quiver,
  As a captive dreamer tosses.

I should turn and rend the cere-clothes round me,
   Giant sinews I should borrow –
Crying, 'O, my brothers, I have also loved her
   In her loneliness and sorrow!

'Let me join with you the jubilant procession;
   Let me chant with you her story;
Then contented I shall go back to the shamrocks,
   Now mine eyes have seen her glory!'

SUSAN K. PHILLIPS

(1831-98?)

Daughter of the Rev. George K. Holdsworth, vicar of Aldborough, West Riding of Yorkshire. In 1856 she married the artist Henry Wyndham Phillips. Many of her verses, some written in Yorkshire dialect, deal with incidents in the lives of the sea coast people of the county. She contributed to most of the better known magazines and journals. Lived latterly at Greenroyd, Ripon.

Ajar

The tiny grain of sand arrests the wheel,
The note that falsely rings spoils all the air;
The drop of poison through the draught will steal,
And leave its work of hidden murder there.

The erring touch the perfect picture blurs,
The careless smile may sting a hope to death;
A pebble flung the lake's whole surface stirs,
The troubled waters crush a root beneath.

And a rash-written word, or spoken jest,
May stop affection's fountain at its source,
Or kill a love that warmed a human breast,
And in its stead leave the grim ache – remorse.

MAY PROBYN
(fl.1875-1909)

Daughter of Julian Probyn of Longhope. A poet and novelist, she lived in London, and was received into the Roman Catholic Church in 1883.

Christmas Carol

Lacking samite and sable,
  Lacking silver and gold,
The Prince Jesus in the poor stable
  Slept, and was three hours old.

As doves by the fair water,
  Mary, not touched of sin,
Sat by Him, – the King's daughter,
  All glorious within.

A lily without one stain, a
  Star where no spot hath room.
Ave, gratia plena –
  Virgo Virginum.

Clad not in pearl-sewn vesture,
  Clad not in cramoisie,
She hath hushed, she hath cradled to rest, her
  God the first time on her knee.

Where is one to adore Him?
  The ox hath dumbly confessed,
With the ass, meek kneeling before Him,
  Et homo factus est.

Not throned on ivory or cedar,
  Not crowned with a Queen's crown,
At her breast it is Mary shall feed her
  Maker, from Heaven come down.

The trees in Paradise blossom
  Sudden, and its bells chime –
She giveth Him, held to her bosom,
  Her immaculate milk the first time.

The night with wings of angels
  Was alight, and its snow-packed ways
Sweet made (say the Evangels)
  With the noise of their virelays.

Quem vidistis, pastores?
  Why go ye feet unshod?
Wot ye within yon door is
  Mary, the Mother of God?

No smoke of spice is ascending
  There – no roses are piled –
But, choicer than all balms blending,
  There Mary hath kissed her child.

Dilectus meus mihi
  Et ego Illi – cold
Small cheek against her cheek, He
  Sleepeth, three hours old.

Love in Mayfair

I must tell you, my dear,
  I'm in love with him, vastly!
Twenty thousand a year,
I must tell you, my dear!
He will soon be a peer –
  And such diamonds! – and, lastly,
I must tell you, my dear,
  I'm in love with him, vastly!

ADELAIDE ANNE PROCTER

(1825-64)

Born in London, eldest child of the poet Bryan Waller Procter. She and two of her sisters became Roman Catholics in 1851. A precocious student, she had a talent for languages, music and painting, and contributed to Charles Dickens's *Household Words* under the pseudonym of Mary Berwick. Philanthropy was the real-life work she had chosen for herself, taking an interest in night schools, sick visiting, and refugees, as well as social questions affecting women. So eagerly did she pursue this kind of activity that her friends became anxious for her health, and eventually she contracted tuberculosis. In 1877 her poetry was as popular in England as Tennyson's. She was the author of the song 'The Lost Chord' as well as many hymns.

Envy

He was the first always: Fortune
  Shone bright in his face.
I fought for years; with no effort
  He conquered the place:
We ran; my feet were all bleeding,
  But he won the race.

Spite of his many successes
  Men loved him the same;
My one pale ray of good fortune
  Met scoffing and blame.
When we erred, they gave him pity,
  But me – only shame.

My home was still in the shadow,
  His lay in the sun:
I longed in vain: what he asked for
  It straightway was done.
Once I staked all my heart's treasure,
  We played – and he won.

Yes; and just now I have seen him,
  Cold, smiling, and blest,
Laid in his coffin. God help me!
  While he is at rest,
I am cursed to live: – even
  Death loved him the best.

From *A Parting*

Without one bitter feeling let us part –
And for the years in which your love has shed
A radiance like a glory round my head
I thank you, yes. I thank you from my heart.

I thank you for the cherished hope of years,
A starry future, dim and yet divine,
Winging its way from Heaven to be mine,
Laden with joy and ignorant of tears.

I thank you, yes. I thank you even more
That my heart learnt not without love to live,
But gave and gave, and still had more to give,
From an abundant and exhaustless store.

I thank you, and no grief is in these tears;
I thank you, not in bitterness but truth,
For the fair vision that adorned my youth
And glorified so many happy years.

I thank you that you taught me the stern truth,
(None other could have told and I believed,)
That vain had been my life, and I deceived,
And wasted all the purpose of my youth.

. . .

I thank you for a terrible awakening,
And if reproach seemed hidden in my pain,
And sorrow seemed to cry on your disdain,
Know that my blessing lay in your forsaking.

A Woman's Question

Before I trust my Fate to thee,
Or place my hand in thine,
Before I let thy Future give
Colour and form to mine,
Before I peril all for thee, question thy soul to-night for me.

I break all slighter bonds, nor feel
A shadow of regret:
Is there one link within the Past,
That holds thy spirit yet?
Or is thy Faith as clear and free as that which I can pledge
to thee?

Does there within thy dimmest dreams
A possible future shine,
Wherein thy life could henceforth breathe,
Untouched, unshared by mine?
If so, at any pain or cost, oh, tell me before all is lost.

Look deeper still. If thou canst feel
Within thy inmost soul,
That thou hast kept a portion back,
While I have staked the whole;
Let no false pity spare the blow, but in true mercy tell me so.

Is there within thy heart a need
That mine cannot fulfil?
One chord that any other hand
Could better wake or still?
Speak now – lest at some future day my whole life wither and
decay.

Lives there within thy nature hid
The demon-spirit Change,
Shedding a passing glory still
On all things new and strange? –
It may not be thy fault alone – but shield my heart against
thy own.

Couldst thou withdraw thy hand one day
And answer to my claim,
That Fate, and that to-day's mistake,
Not thou – had been to blame?
Some soothe their conscience thus: but thou, wilt surely
warn and save me now.

Nay, answer *not* – I dare not hear,
The words would come too late;
Yet I would spare thee all remorse,
So, comfort thee, my Fate –
Whatever on my heart may fall – remember I *would* risk
it all!

A Woman's Answer

I will not let you say a Woman's part
Must be to give exclusive love alone;
Dearest, although I love you so, my heart
Answers a thousand claims besides your own.

I love – what do I not love? earth and air
Find space within my heart, and myriad things
You would not deign to heed, are cherished there,
And vibrate on its very inmost strings.

I love the summer with her ebb and flow
Of light, and warmth, and music that have nurst
Her tender buds to blossoms... and you know
It was in summer that I saw you first.

I love the winter dearly too,... but then
I owe it so much; on a winter's day,
Bleak, cold, and stormy, you returned again,
When you had been those weary months away.

I love the Stars like friends; so many nights
  I gazed at them, when you were far from me,
Till I grew blind with tears . . . those far off lights
  Could watch you, whom I longed in vain to see.

I love the Flowers; happy hours lie
  Shut up within their petals close and fast:
You have forgotten, dear: but they and I
  Keep every fragment of the golden Past.

. . .

I love all those who love you; all who owe
  Comfort to you: and I can find regret
Even for those poorer hearts who once could know,
  And once could love you, and can now forget.

Well, is my heart so narrow – I, who spare
  Love for all these? Do I not even hold
My favourite books in special tender care,
  And prize them as a miser does his gold?

The Poets that you used to read to me
  While summer twilights faded in the sky;
But most of all I think Aurora Leigh,
  Because – because – do you remember why?

Will you be jealous? Did you guess before
  I loved so many things? – Still you the best: –
Dearest, remember that I love you more,
  Oh, more a thousand times than all the rest!

DOLLIE RADFORD
(1858-1920)

Born in Worcester, the daughter of a London West End tailor named Maitland. She published several volumes of verse and stories, and a verse play. She and her husband, Ernest Radford, poet, art historian and critic, knew Eleanor Marx, William Morris and many of the leading literary figures of the day, including George Bernard Shaw and D.H. Lawrence. Most of her married life was spent in Hammersmith and Hampstead, London. She had three children.

Chrysanthemums

November with mysterious feet
    Creeps slowly through the land,
And on the bridge and in the street,
Amid the town's tumultuous beat,
    Spreads out a quiet hand,
And wraps around us unaware
    His mantle grey and cold;
But he has blossoms still to spare:
We find fresh flowers rich and rare
    Hid in each misty fold.

Soliloquy of a Maiden Aunt

The ladies bow, and partners set,
And turn around and pirouette
        And trip the Lancers.

But no one seeks my ample chair,
Or asks me with persuasive air
        To join the dancers.

They greet me, as I sit alone
Upon my solitary throne,
        And pass politely.

Yet mine could keep the measured beat,
As surely as the youngest feet,
And tread as lightly.

No other maiden had my skill
In our old homestead on the hill –
That merry May-time.

When Allan closed the flagging ball,
And danced with me before them all,
Until the day-time.

Again I laugh, and step alone,
And curtsey low as on my own
His strong hand closes.

But Allan now seeks staid delight,
His son there, brought my niece to-night
These early roses.

Time orders well, we have our Spring,
Our songs, and may-flower gathering,
Our love and laughter.

And children chatter all the while,
And leap the brook and climb the stile
And follow after.

And yet – the step of Allan's son,
Is not as light as was the one
That went before it.

And that old lace, I think, falls down
Less softly on Priscilla's gown
Than when I wore it.

Two Songs

Winds blow cold in the bright March weather,
  Yet I heard her sing in the street to-day,
And the tattered garments scarce hung together
  Round her tiny form as she turned away.
She was too little to know or care
Why she and her mother were singing there.

Skies are fair when the buds are springing,
  When the March sun rises up fresh and strong,
And a little maid, with her mother singing,
  Smiled in my face as she skipped along.
She was too happy to wonder why
She laughed and sang as she passed me by.

Stars are bright, and the moon rejoices
  To pierce the clouds with her broken light,
But the air is heavy with childish voices,
  Two songs ring through the clear March night –
Songs which the night with burning tears
Sings out again to the coming years.

AGNES MARY FRANCES ROBINSON

(1857-1944)

Born in Leamington, Warwickshire, daughter of the archdiaconal architect for Coventry. Her girlhood was spent in Warwickshire and Lancashire but she was educated in Belgium and Italy, and pursued literary and classical studies at University College, London. At the age of twenty-one she was given the choice of a ball or publication of her poems in book form, and chose the latter. She was married twice, first to the oriental scholar James Darmesteter, then to Pierre Emile Duclaux. In addition to verse she wrote a novel, and biographies of Emily Brontë, Froissart, and Victor Hugo.

Princesses

How did they feel, I wonder?
    Fairy princesses, –
Sending their lovers through
Danger as strange as new;
Caves full of flame and thunder,
    Fierce wildernesses?

I, of a simpler mind,
    Own them above me.
Dear, I could never ask
You for the lightest task –
So do I dread to find
    You may not love me!

Thanksgiving for Flowers

You bring me flowers – behold my shaded room
Is grown all glorious and alive with Light.
Moonshine of pallid primroses, and bright
Daffodil-suns that light the way of the tomb.
You bring me dreams – through sleep's close-lidded gloom,
Sad violets mourn for Sappho all the night,

Where purple saffrons make antique delight
Mid crown'd memorials of Narcissus' doom.
A scent of herbs now sets me musing on
Men dead i' the fennel-beds on Marathon,
My flowers, my dreams and I shall lie as dead!
Flowers fade, dreams wake, men die; but never dies
The soul whereby these things were perfected, –
This leaves the world on flower with memories.

CHRISTINA ROSSETTI

(1830-94)

Born in London, the younger daughter of Gabriele Rossetti, Professor of Italian at King's College, London. She was educated at home, and her first poetry was published when she was twelve. Her work appeared under the name of Ellen Alleyne in 1850 with that of her brother Dante Gabriel in the Pre-Raphaelite Brotherhood's journal *The Germ*. One of the greatest and most spiritual of English poets, and a devout High Church Anglican, her life was a retiring one, spent largely in caring for her mother who lived until 1886, and in religious duties. She twice rejected proposals of marriage, breaking her engagements to the painter James Collinson and later to the translator Charles Bagot Cayley. In 1873 she contracted Graves' disease and retreated into invalidism, becoming almost a recluse. Even so, she was much concerned with such social issues as poverty, prostitution and unemployment. She is buried at Highgate Cemetery.

A Dirge

Why were you born when the snow was falling?
You should have come to the cuckoo's calling,
Or when grapes are green in the cluster,
Or at least when lithe swallows muster
    For their far off flying
    From summer dying.

Why did you die when the lambs were cropping?
You should have died at the apples' dropping,
When the grasshopper comes to trouble,
And the wheat-fields are sodden stubble,
    And all winds go sighing
    For sweet things dying.

From the Antique

It's a weary life, it is, she said –
   Doubly blank in a woman's lot:
I wish and I wish I were a man:
   Or, better than any being, were not:

Were nothing at all in all the world,
   Not a body and not a soul:
Not so much as a grain of dust
   Or drop of water from pole to pole.

Still the world would wag on the same,
   Still the seasons go and come:
Blossoms bloom as in days of old,
   Cherries ripen and wild bees hum.

None would miss me in all the world,
   How much less would care or weep:
I should be nothing, while all the rest
   Would wake and weary and fall asleep.

Memory

I

I nursed it in my bosom while it lived,
   I hid it in my heart when it was dead;
In joy I sat alone, even so I grieved
   Alone and nothing said.

I shut the door to face the naked truth,
   I stood alone – I faced the truth alone,
Stripped bare of self-regard or forms or ruth
   Till first and last were shown.

I took the perfect balances and weighed;
   No shaking of my hand disturbed the poise;
Weighed, found it wanting: not a word I said,
   But silent made my choice.

None know the choice I made; I make it still.
  None know the choice I made and broke my heart,
Breaking mine idol: I have braced my will
  Once, chosen for once my part.

I broke it at a blow, I laid it cold,
  Crushed in my deep heart where it used to live.
My heart dies inch by inch; the time grows old,
  Grows old in which I grieve.

II

I have a room whereinto no one enters
  Save I myself alone:
  There sits a blessed memory on a throne,
There my life centres.

While winter comes and goes – oh tedious comer! –
  And while its nip-wind blows;
  While bloom the bloodless lily and warm rose
Of lavish summer.

If any should force entrance he might see there
  One buried yet not dead,
  Before whose face I no more bow my head
Or bend my knee there;

But often in my worn life's autumn weather
  I watch there with clear eyes,
  And think how it will be in Paradise
When we're together.

Monna Innominata

Vien dietro a me e lascia dir le genti. DANTE
Contando i casi della vita nostra. PETRARCA

Many in aftertimes will say of you
'He loved her' – while of me what will they say?
   Not that I loved you more than just in play,
For fashion's sake as idle women do.
Even let them prate; who know not what we knew
   Of love and parting in exceeding pain,
   Of parting hopeless here to meet again,
Hopeless on earth, and heaven is out of view.
But by my heart of love laid bare to you,
   My love that you can make not void nor vain,
Love that foregoes you but to claim anew
      Beyond this passage of the gate of death,
   I charge you at the Judgment make it plain
      My love of you was life and not a breath.

A Pause of Thought

I looked for that which is not, nor can be,
   And hope deferred made my heart sick in truth:
   But years must pass before a hope of youth
      Is resigned utterly.

I watched and waited with a steadfast will:
   And though the object seemed to flee away
   That I so longed for, ever day by day
      I watched and waited still.

Sometimes I said: This thing shall be no more;
   My expectation wearies and shall cease;
   I will resign it now and be at peace:
      Yet never gave it o'er.

Sometimes I said: It is an empty name
   I long for; to a name why should I give
   The peace of all the days I have to live? –
      Yet gave it all the same.

Alas, thou foolish one! alike unfit
   For healthy joy and salutary pain:
   Thou knowest the chase useless, and again
      Turnest to follow it.

Rest

O Earth, lie heavily upon her eyes;
   Seal her sweet eyes weary of watching, Earth;
   Lie close around her; leave no room for mirth
With its harsh laughter, nor for sound of sighs.
She hath no questions, she hath no replies,
   Hushed in and curtained with a blessèd dearth
   Of all that irked her from the hour of birth;
With stillness that is almost Paradise.
Darkness more clear than noon-day holdeth her,
   Silence more musical than any song;
Even her very heart has ceased to stir:
Until the morning of Eternity
Her rest shall not begin nor end, but be;
   And when she wakes she will not think it long.

Spring

Frost-locked all the winter,
Seeds, and roots, and stones of fruits,
What shall make their sap ascend
That they may put forth shoots?
Tips of tender green,
Leaf, or blade, or sheath;
Telling of the hidden life
That breaks forth underneath,
Life nursed in its grave by Death.

Blows the thaw-wind pleasantly,
Drips the soaking rain,
By fits looks down the waking sun:
Young grass springs on the plain;
Young leaves clothe early hedgerow trees;
Seeds, and roots, and stones of fruits,
Swollen with sap put forth their shoots;
Curled-headed ferns sprout in the lane;
Birds sing and pair again.

There is no time like Spring,
When life's alive in everything,
Before new nestlings sing,
Before cleft swallows speed their journey back
Along the trackless track –
God guides their wing,
He spreads their table that they nothing lack, –
Before the daisy grows a common flower,
Before the sun has power
To scorch the world up in his noontide hour.

There is no time like Spring,
Like Spring that passes by;
There is no life like Spring-life born to die, –
Piercing the sod,
Clothing the uncouth clod,
Hatched in the nest,
Fledged on the windy bough,
Strong on the wing:
There is no time like Spring that passes by,
Now newly born, and now
Hastening to die.

Twice

I took my heart in my hand
  (O my love, O my love),
I said: let me fall or stand,
  Let me live or die,

But this once hear me speak –
  (O my love, O my love) –
Yet a woman's words are weak:
  You should speak, not I.

You took my heart in your hand
  With a friendly smile,
With a critical eye you scanned,
  Then set it down,
And said: It is still unripe,
  Better wait awhile;
Wait while the skylarks pipe,
  Till the corn grows brown.

As you set it down it broke –
  Broke, but I did not wince;
I smiled at the speech you spoke,
  At your judgment that I heard:
But I have not often smiled
  Since then, nor questioned since,
Nor cared for corn-flowers wild,
  Nor sung with the singing bird.

I take my heart in my hand,
  O my God, O my God,
My broken heart in my hand:
  Thou hast seen, judge Thou.
My hope was written on sand,
  O my God, O my God:
Now let Thy judgment stand –
  Yea, judge me now.

This contemned of a man,
  This marred one heedless day,
This heart take Thou to scan
  Both within and without:
Refine with fire its gold,
  Purge Thou its dross away –
Yea, hold it in Thy hold,
  Whence none can pluck it out.

I take my heart in my hand –
   I shall not die, but live –
Before Thy face I stand;
   I, for Thou callest such:
All that I have I bring,
   All that I am I give,
Smile Thou and I shall sing,
   But shall not question much.

Where Shall I Find a White Rose Blowing?

Where shall I find a white rose blowing?
      'Out in the garden where all sweets be'.
But out in my garden the snow was snowing
      And never a white rose opened for me.
Nought but snow and a wind were blowing
And snowing.

Where shall I find a blush rose blushing?
      'On the garden wall or the garden bed'.
But out in my garden the rain was rushing
      And never a blush rose raised its head.
Nothing glowing, flushing or blushing;
Rain rushing.

Where shall I find a red rose budding?
      'Out in the garden where all things grow'.
But out in my garden a flood was flooding,
      And never a red rose began to blow.
Out in the flooding what should be budding?
All flooding!

Now is winter and now is sorrow,
      No roses but only thorns to-day:
Thorns will put on roses to-morrow
      Winter and sorrow scudding away.
No more winter and no more sorrow
To-morrow.

DORA SIGERSON SHORTER
(1866-1918)

Born in Dublin. Her father was a surgeon and Gaelic scholar, her mother a writer. She was educated at home in a cultured atmosphere. Her first talent was for drawing, and she was in her twenties before she began to write. Like her greatest friends, Katherine Tynan and the American Louise Imogen Guiney, she was a Roman Catholic. In 1896 she married the journalist and critic Clement Shorter and settled in London. The marriage was very happy but being fervently patriotic she always felt an exile in England. At her country home in Buckinghamshire she busied herself in gardening, and took up sculpture, for which she had a real gift, without any training. After the Easter Rebellion of 1916 she worked on behalf of the accused and the imprisoned. She carved the memorial sculpture group of the Irish patriots in Dublin Cemetery, where she herself is buried.

Gray Eyes

Sitting alone in my room,
Alone in the gathering gloom,
Solitude in the rest of the tomb.
While the drip, drip, drip of the rain,
Like tears that are falling in vain
For a loss that is gone past regain,
Falls soft on the window-pane
Of my room.

Alone, alone, alone,
And no one to hear my moan
In the world's great heart of stone;
Only poverty that wakes disgust,
Only promises light as dust,
And nought that is true or just,
Cold hearts that you cannot trust –
Alone.

Weary of hopes that fade,
Of a life that is one long shade
Of joys that bloom decayed,
Fall cool on my heart, O rain

Till you soften this bitter pain,
This ice that doth it enchain –
Oh, let it once hope again,
Or fade.

Ye who in the crowd pass by,
Not giving a glance or a sigh,
Not heeding my lonely cry,
Oh, pause, and say, ere you go,
Is there love in that world you know?
You have caused me all my woe,
Gray eyes, gray eyes, ah! so
Pass by.

The Gypsies' Road

I shall go on the gypsies' road,
   The road that has no ending;
For the sedge is brown on the lone lake side,
   The wild geese eastward tending.

I shall go as the unfetter'd wave,
   From shore to shore, forgetting
The grief that lies 'neath a roof-tree's shade,
   The years that bring regretting.

No law shall dare my wandering stay,
   No man my acres measure;
The world was made for the gypsies' feet,
   The winding road for pleasure.

And I shall drift as the pale leaf stray'd,
   Whither the wild wind listed,
I shall sleep in the dark of the hedge,
   'Neath rose and thorn entwisted.

This was a call in the heart of the night,
   A whispering dream's dear treasure:
'The world was made for the nomads' feet,
   The winding road for pleasure.'

I stole at dawn from my roof-tree's shade,
  And the cares that it did cover;
I flew to the heart of the fierce north wind,
  As a maid will greet her lover.

But a thousand hands did draw me back
  And bid me to their tending;
I may not go on the gypsies' road –
  The road that has no ending.

In Wintry Weather

Dear, in wintry weather,
How close we crept together!
The storms, with all their thunder,
Could not our fond hands sunder.
No sorrow followed after,
Cold words or scornful laughter.
How close we crept together,
Through all the wintry weather!

Dear, when each rose uncurled
To its sweet narrow world,
You went to cull their glory;
You would not hear my story,
Too sweet the birds were singing,
Too fair the buds were swinging.
If I should come or go
You did not care to know.

When each sweet rose uncurled
To its unknown world,
How could you e'er remember
That in a bleak December,
Through all the bitter weather
We crept so close together.

ELIZABETH (LIZZIE) SIDDAL
(1843-62)

Born in London. Her father, a Sheffield cutler, had moved with his family to the Newington Butts area of London before her birth. After receiving a basic education she became an assistant in a bonnet shop close to Leicester Square. She was a beautiful girl, tall with a fine carriage and a mass of coppery-gold hair. Walter Howell Deverell, a young painter who associated with members of the Pre-Raphaelite Brotherhood, noticed her in the shop and introduced her to Dante Gabriel Rossetti. She and Rossetti were married in 1860 and settled in London. The marriage was not a happy one but under her husband's guidance Lizzie began to draw and paint and at times sat for him. Her health was extremely bad – she was consumptive and had difficulty in retaining food. A stillborn female child was delivered in 1861. On 10th February 1862 she died from an overdose of laudanum.

Dead Love

Oh never weep for love that's dead
   Since love is seldom true
But changes his fashion from blue to red,
   From brightest red to blue,
And love was born to an early death
   And is so seldom true.

Then harbour no smile on your bonny face
   To win the deepest sigh.
The fairest words on truest lips
   Pass on and surely die,
And you will stand alone, my dear,
   When wintry winds draw nigh.

Sweet, never weep for what cannot be,
   For this God has not given.
If the merest dream of love were true
   Then, sweet, we should be in heaven,
And this is only earth, my dear,
   Where true love is not given.

Worn Out

Thy strong arms are round me, love,
My head is on thy breast;
Low words of comfort come from thee
Yet my soul has no rest

For I am but a startled thing
Nor can I ever be
Aught save a bird whose broken wing
Must fly away from thee.

I cannot give to thee the love
I gave so long ago,
The love that turned and struck me down
Amid the blinding snow.

I can but give a failing heart
And weary eyes of pain,
A faded mouth that cannot smile
And may not laugh again.

Yet keep thine arms around me, love,
Until I fall asleep;
Then leave me, saying no goodbye
Lest I might wake, and weep.

A Year and a Day

I lie among the tall green grass
That bends above my head
And covers up my wasted face
And folds me in its bed
Tenderly and lovingly
Like grass above the dead.

Dim phantoms of an unknown ill
Float through my tired brain;
The unformed visions of my life
Pass by in ghostly train;
Some pause to touch me on the cheek,
Some scatter tears like rain.

. . .

The river ever running down
Between its grassy bed
The voices of a thousand birds
That clang above my head,
Shall bring to me a sadder dream
When this sad dream is dead.

A silence falls upon my heart
And hushes all its pain.
I stretch my hands in the long grass
And fall to sleep again,
There to lie empty of all love
Like beaten corn of grain.

MENELLA BUTE SMEDLEY
(1820-77)

Born in Great Marlow, Buckinghamshire, the daughter of a clergyman. She was privately educated at home but little is known of her life apart from her writing. She never married, and was especially interested and active in the welfare of orphan and pauper children. Her publications include several volumes of verse and a five-act poetic drama entitled *Lady Grace*, which remained unacted.

Wind Me a Summer Crown

'Wind me a summer crown,' she said,
  'And set it on my brows;
For I must go, while I am young,
  Home to my Father's house.

'And make me ready for the day,
  And let me not be stay'd;
I would not linger on the way
  As if I was afraid.

'O, will the golden courts of heaven,
  When I have paced them o'er,
Be lovely as the lily walks
  Which I must see no more?

'And will the seraph hymns and harps,
  When they have fill'd my ear,
Be tender as my mother's voice,
  Which I must never hear?

'And shall I like where sunsets drift,
  Or where the stars are born,
Or where the living tints are mixt
  To paint the clouds of morn?'

Your mother's tones shall reach you still,
  Even sweeter than they were;
And the false love that broke your heart
  Shall be forgotten there:

And not a star or flower is born
   The beauty of that shore;
There is a face which you shall see
   And wish for nothing more.

EMMELINE STUART-WORTLEY
(1806-55)

Third daughter of the 5th Duke of Rutland. In 1831 she married the Hon. Charles Stuart-Wortley, brother of Lord Wharncliffe. They had two sons and one daughter. She published many volumes of verse, several plays, accounts of her travels in the United States and Portugal, and edited *The Keepsake* in 1837 and 1840. On a visit to the Middle East in 1855 she had her leg fractured by the kick of a mule whilst riding near Jerusalem. She persisted in undertaking the journey from Beirut to Aleppo but, despite medical attention, she was so weakened and exhausted that she died on her return to Beirut.

Sonnet

Child of my heart, would I could now behold
   Thy face of infant purity and grace;
   That opening, wakening, brightening, flowering face,
And in a mother's fond embrace enfold.
Though sweetly, smilingly, the hours have rolled
   Since I have seen thee – yet the time, the space
   Have oft been lengthened, widened on the race
Of hours, by fond regrets, all uncontrolled.
   My child, my children, oh! to see again
Those infant features, stamped upon my mind,
   Whose dear and blessed memory is a pain.
Then were I happy, happiest, but entwined
   With grief must recollection still remain,
Till I once more, in joy, my living treasures find.

ROSE ELLEN THACKERAY

Youngest daughter of Captain John Robinson of the Scots Guards. Married the Rev. Thackeray of Horstead Rectory, Norfolk. Her son Arthur T.J. Thackeray, born 1852, eventually became vicar of Norton Subcourse, Norfolk. Her *Social Sketches in Verse* was published by T. Cautley Newby in London, 1868.

A Leaf from the Diary of Lady Constance

Belgravia, 1868.

May 1st.

Awoke at eight, had tea in bed;
Rested once more my aching head.
Not home till four, no rest till five;
I wonder that I am alive!
Got up and dressed, seedy and slow,
Ordered my horse for Rotten Row;
Flirted and galloped there till two,
Then lunched, and pondered what to do.
Early carriage at half past four;
Oh! shopping is a horrid bore!
Dropped some pasteboards on the way;
Drove to the park so full and gay.
Talked to Sir Battered – quite a list
Of games he won last night at whist!
Yawn'd and drove home, dress number three;
Bennet brought up a cup of tea.
Carriage again, rolled out to dine;
Which meal commenced at half-past nine.
At twelve behold me on the road
To Lady Scamper's grand abode.
Showed myself there, then off once more;
Danced and got home by half-past four.

May 2nd.

Awoke, planned 'Croquet' in the Square,
To make young Singleton declare!

Arose at ten, tried a new hat,
Methought the feathers hung too flat!
The golden hair dye suits me well,
I thought of Atkins in Pall Mall.
Mem.: dropped my chignon in the ride;
I wondered why my 'Janette' shied,
But knew I could not be betrayed,
As all young ladies wear *one shade!*
Wrote invitations for a ball.
Young Singleton then came to call;
Goes to the Opera to-night
Rushed up and dressed! in real delight,
Heard Sinico and Titians sing;
Then for two balls was on the wing,
Arrived at home by half-past three!
Young Singleton's declared to me!

Receipt for a Head

Take a head which wears no bonnet,
A head with lots of hair upon it.
The head, though neither young nor old,
Must then be dyed a splendid gold;
Then take a brush and scrub it round,
Until no silken spot is found,
Then draw it backwards through a hedge
Till ev'ry hair stands out on edge;
Then turn the ends to make them curl,
And ornament with flower and pearl.
The head, when it goes out, must wear
A hat in shape to make you stare.
A rabbit, pheasant, or a wren,
Sewn to the brim, must stare again;
While two bright eyes complete the charm.
They may do good, they may do harm;
But be they black or blue as Heaven,
Heads have bright eyes in sixty-seven.

ROSE HAIG THOMAS

Her collection of lyrical poems entitled *Pan* was published by Bliss, Sands & Co. in London, 1897. She was also the author of a book on designing stone gardens, published in 1905.

Odelet
To My Green Tree Frog
on a Sunny Spring Morning

He too, then, would away to seek his kind!
Cold blooded! Nay, the spring throbs in his veins,
Poor prisoner! The way he cannot find,
And must in solitude endure his pains,
A pickle jar his melancholy lot,
A pinch of moss, a piece of virgin cork,
A dried and broken twig to climb. Ah, not
For him the balmy airs the March sun's work,
And not for him spiced buds their cases toss!
He shed his winter garment all the same
And made him smart with coat of emerald gloss;
Ah, where the fair that might these beauties claim?
His tiny hands in supplication spread
Upon the glass that walls his hermit bed
Appeal for freedom, while his orange throat
Is roundly swelling with a pleading note.
The insects flit before him to and fro,
Their buzzing whets his rising appetite.
His cruel captor will not let him go
But doth instead these lines to him indite.

GRACE TOLLEMACHE

(1869-1925?)

Daughter of the 2nd Baron Tollemache who was M.P. for West Cheshire, 1872-85. Her mother was the daughter of the 9th Earl of Galloway. The Tollemache family owned large estates in Cheshire, including Dorfold Hall, Nantwich, and Peckforton Castle, Tarporley. Their London home was at 40 Cadogan Gardens, S.W.

To Her Gown
(on laying it by)

Dear gown, that he has known me in –
  And still perhaps his eyes would trace –
You're blameless, though I could not win
  His love – yours was a faultless grace!

For so much folly to confess
  I chose you wistfully, with care,
Because I think much comeliness
  Accrues from comely clothes we wear.

I warrant you became me well –
  At once we seemed so long allied,
And by the way your rich folds fell,
  To do me honour seemed your pride.

I wonder you should still seem new,
  For though indeed if they be told,
The times I wore you were but few,
  My heart in the same while grew old;

And as clothes' fashions so soon change,
  And not the comeliest long remain,
Next year you'd be considered strange –
  But you shall not be worn again.

You never shall provoke the scoff
   Of fools at antiquated worth;
Nor, now that I have left you off,
   Be cast to beggars of mean birth.

But in the chest where you must lie
   Myself I'll lay you, like a friend;
For with you, must be now put by
   Those dreams that had so soon an end!

KATHARINE TYNAN
(1861-1931)

Born at Clondalkin, County Dublin, the daughter of a farmer. A Roman Catholic, she was educated at Siena Convent, Drogheda, and began writing at the age of seventeen. A poet and prose writer, she was a leading member of the Celtic literary revival and a friend of Yeats, Parnell, the Meynells and the Rossettis. In 1883 she married Henry A. Hinkson, a lawyer. They first made their home in London but later moved to County Mayo when he was appointed a resident magistrate. She wrote more than a hundred novels and also published a series of autobiographical works.

On a Birthday

Shall I lament my vanished spring?
Ah, no, its joys went withering:
Its hopes, long sick, decayed and died
With its desires unsatisfied:
A moaning wind of discontent
Stripped the young boughs of bloom and scent;
The rain was raining every day.

Now though it be no longer May,
O heart, what youth renewed is ours!
With generous scarcely hoped-for flowers.
And the good summer but begun:
With longer days and riper sun,
And the large possibilities
Of gifts and grace and good increase
In the rich weather yet to come.

Nor shall the autumn strike us dumb
Who knows what fruit for us shall be
Swung in some ruddy-hearted tree;
What hopes shall find their harvesting
When outward birds are on the wing;
When pale September lights her fire –
Her Will-o'-the-Wisp on every briar –
What ship shall sail to shore at last?

Nor shall we dread the winter blast
On the long evening of our year
With nothing more to hope or fear:
Looking to keep Christ's festival,
In His own fair and lighted hall.
And the longest night is done,
Cometh the Christmas benison.

Slow Spring

O year, grow slowly. Exquisite, holy,
  The days go on
With almonds showing the pink stars blowing,
  And birds in the dawn.

Grow slowly, year, like a child that is dear,
  Or a lamb that is mild,
By little steps, and by little skips,
  Like a lamb or a child.

MARGARET VELEY
(1843-87)

Born at Braintree, Essex, the second of the four daughters of Augustus Charles Veley, of Swiss descent, who practised as a solicitor in the town. Her mother, Sophia, was the daughter of the Rev. Thomas Ludbey, rector of Cranham. Margaret was educated at home by governesses but spent one term at Queen's College, Tufnell Park, becoming a good French scholar. She was successful in getting her poems and stories published in *Blackwood's Magazine, Macmillan's Magazine* and other journals, and she moved to London in 1880. Two of her sisters and her father died between 1877 and 1885, and these bereavements strongly affected her later writing. Interested in many things besides literature, she was a very shy person and completely free from vanity.

Mother and Child

Bitter blasts and vapours dim –
What had they to do with him?
Spring, though she was far away,
Took dominion for a day,
Filled the air with breathings soft,
Bade a skylark sing aloft,
When we laid him in his bed,
Cloudless blue above his head.

It was not for him to reach
Manly height, and thought, and speech,
Not to climb untrodden steeps,
Not to search out unknown deeps,
Not through warring joy and pain
Kingliness of soul to gain.

He had only baby words,
Little music, like the birds,
Sweetly inarticulate,
Nothing wise, nor high, nor great.
Sunny smiles and kisses sweet –
White and softly childish feet –
Curls that floated on the breeze –
We remember him for these.

They are weary who are wise.
He looked up with happy eyes,
Little knowing, little seeing,
Only praising God by being.

Oh, the life we could not save!
Do not say, above his grave,
That the fair and darling face
Was but lent a little space
Till the Father called him back,
By an unknown homeward track.
No, though Death came darkly chill –
Bade the beating heart be still,
Touching him with fingers cold –
What was given still we hold;
Though he died, as die the flowers,
He for evermore is ours.

Ours, though we must travel soon
Onward through Life's afternoon;
Shadows, falling long and grey,
Gather round the western day,
And our twilight visions show
How the years shall come and go.

Little maids, with tangled curls,
Change to slender, dreamy girls;
Chubby rogues grow tall, and then
Go their way as bearded men.
And the mother stands aside,
With an ache beneath her pride,
And a sorrow 'mid her joys,
For the vanished babes and boys;
So the earlier gladness wanes –
But the little one remains.

For a house that once has known
Tiny feet on stair and stone –
Steps that never more shall sound,
Feet at rest beneath the ground –
Keeps remembrance of the dead,
And the music of their tread.

Not at noonday, busy, bright,
Only in the quiet night,
With a thrill of sweetest pain,
Comes that music once again,
Heard in stillness and apart
Echoed from his mother's heart.

A Student

For him the past has poured her drowsy wine;
   And, turning from all beauty 'neath the sun,
Ever he seeks the dim horizon line,
   Regions afar, where earth and sky are one.
Here, in this central moment of to-day,
High heaven seems so very far away.

Sadness there is, not sorrow, on his brow,
   He shrinks alike from laughter and from tears,
When happier glances hail the budding bough,
   He tracks the footsteps of departed years,
Where, faintly dim, their memories linger yet
All grown about with moss and violet.

His fellow men our student little heeds;
   His pathway lies 'mid visionary throngs –
Spring, though he meets her in the daisied meads,
   Lives for him only in her ancient songs;
Nay, very Love himself he does but know
A boy, with bow and arrows, long ago.

He cannot feel for human hopes and fears,
   All hopes and fears are chronicled for him,
Unnoticed glides his little span of years,
   His eyes are fixed on ages vast and dim.
He dreams of bygone days, with thoughtful brow,
Till Life stands still, and, startled, whispers 'Now!'

AUGUSTA WEBSTER

(1837-94)

Born at Poole, Dorset. Her father, Vice-Admiral George Davies, held various Coast Guard commands. Her earliest years were spent on board the *Griper* in Chichester Harbour. The family later resided for six years in Banff Castle and she attended school in Banff. When her father became Chief Constable of Cambridgeshire in 1851 they moved to Cambridge, where she went to classes at the School of Art. During brief stays in Paris and Geneva she acquired a full knowledge of French, and subsequently studied Greek, Italian and Spanish. From 1860 she published novels under the pseudonym Cecil Home. In 1863 she married Thomas Webster, a Fellow of Trinity College and law lecturer, who later practised as a solicitor in London. She was a strong advocate of universal education and was twice elected to the London School Board, representing the Chelsea area. Always interested in the advancement of women, some of her essays were reprinted by the Women's Suffrage Society.

Mother and Daughter

Sometimes, as young things will, she vexes me,
    Wayward, or too unheeding, or too blind.
    Like aimless birds that, flying on a wind,
Strike slant against their own familiar tree;
Like venturous children pacing with the sea,
    That turn but when the breaker spurts behind
Outreaching them with spray: she in such kind
Is borne against some fault, or does not flee.

And so, may be, I blame her for her wrong,
    And she will frown and lightly plead her part,
And then I bid her go. But 'tis not long:
    Then comes she lip to ear and heart to heart.
And thus forgiven her love seems newly strong,
    And, oh my penitent, how dear thou art!

Not to Be

The rose said 'Let but this long rain be past,
  And I shall feel my sweetness in the sun
And pour its fulness into life at last.'
    But when the rain was done,
But when the dawn sparkled through unclouded air,
    She was not there.

The lark said 'Let but winter be away,
  And blossoms come, and light, and I will soar,
And lose the earth, and be the voice of day.'
    But when the snows were o'er,
But when spring broke in blueness overhead,
    The lark was dead.

And myriad roses made the garden glow,
  And skylarks carolled all the summer long –
What lack of birds to sing and flowers to blow?
    Yet, ah, lost scent, lost song!
Poor empty rose, poor lark that never trilled!
    Dead unfulfilled!

Seeds

Seeds with wings between earth and sky
    Fluttering, flying;
  Seeds of a lily with blood-red core
  Breathing of myrrh and of giroflore:
Where winds drop them there must they lie,
    Living or dying.

Some to the garden, some to the wall,
    Fluttering, falling;
  Some to the river, some to earth:
  Those that reach the right soil get birth;
None of the rest have lived at all –
    Whose voice is calling:

'Here is soil for winged seeds that near,
        Fluttering, fearing,
    Where they shall root and burgeon and spread.
    Lacking the heart-room the song lies dead:
Half is the song that reaches the ear,
        Half is the hearing'?

JANE FRANCESCA WILDE, Lady Wilde

(1826-96)

Daughter of Archdeacon Elgee. In 1851 she married Sir William R.W. Wilde, the distinguished surgeon and Irish antiquary who became President of the Irish Academy. Their son was Oscar Wilde, the dramatist and wit. For many years her salon was the most famous in Dublin. Her verse was published under the pseudonym 'Speranza' as well as her own name. She was the author of *Ancient Cures, Charms, and Usages of Ireland* and similar prose works. Her last years were spent in London, overwhelmed by poverty, bereavement and other troubles.

From *The Famine Year*

Weary men, what reap ye? – Golden corn for the stranger.
What sow ye? – Human corses that wait for the avenger.
Fainting forms, hunger-stricken, what see you in the offing?
Stately ships to bear our food away, amid the stranger's scoffing.
There's a proud array of soldiers – what do they round your door?
They guard our masters' granaries from the thin hands of the poor.
Pale mothers, wherefore weeping? – Would to God that we were
dead –
Our children swoon before us, and we cannot give them bread.

Little children, tears are strange upon your infant faces,
God meant you but to smile within your mother's soft embraces.
Oh! we know not what is smiling, and we know not what is dying;
But we're hungry, very hungry, and we cannot stop our crying.
And some of us grow cold and white – we know not what it means;
But, as they lie beside us, we tremble in our dreams.
There's a gaunt crowd on the highway – are ye come to pray to man,
With hollow eyes that cannot weep, and for words your faces wan?

No; the blood is dead within our veins – we care not now for life;
Let us die hid in the ditches, far from children and from wife;
We cannot stay and listen to their raving, famished cries –
Bread! Bread! Bread! and none to still their agonies.
We left our infants playing with their dead mother's hand:
We left our maidens maddened by the fever's scorching brand:
Better, maiden, thou wert strangled in thy own dark-twisted tresses –
Better, infant, thou wert smothered in thy mother's first caresses.

. . .

We are wretches, famished, scorned, human tools to build your
pride,
But God will yet take vengeance for the souls for whom Christ died.
Now is your hour of pleasure – bask ye in the world's caress;
But our whitening bones against ye will arise as witnesses,
From the cabins and the ditches, in their charred, uncoffin'd masses,
For the Angel of the Trumpet will know them as he passes.
A ghastly, spectral army, before the great God we'll stand,
And arraign ye as our murderers, the spoilers of our land.

SARAH (SADIE) WILLIAMS

(1841-68)

Born in London, the only child of a wealthy father of Welsh extraction. She was educated at home by governesses before attending Queen's College. One of her tutors was Edward Hayes Plumptre, Dean of Wells, the poet and hymn writer, who encouraged her literary ambitions. She had a particular gift in writing for children. Thanks to her father's success and her own earning power as a writer, she was able to live the life of a student and author, donating half her earnings to the poor.

Fault-Finding

(Margaret.)

Some one said,
He is no friend who will not tell my faults.
And so I sat me down to look for thine,
To mark the sable flaws that fleck thine ermine.

I found a scorn unwise for things ignoble,
A power of silent wrath consuming wrong,
A way of digging deep below the sunshine,
A doubt of self, and trust in other men;
I said, 'These are thy follies.'

I found a habit of self-sacrifice,
A tardy vision of rights personal,
A way of stepping back from thrusting crowds,
A loose light hold of things material;
I said, 'There thou art wrong.'

I found, – but lo! the thorns are blossoming!
It is a sacred rod my hand hath touched;
Who counts the petals of a passion-flower?
I know thy faults, dear, and they are thy crown.

Youth and Maidenhood

Like a drop of water is my heart
  Laid upon her soft and rosy palm,
Turned whichever way her hand doth turn,
  Trembling in an ecstasy of calm.

Like a broken rose-leaf is my heart,
  Held within her close and burning clasp,
Breathing only dying sweetness out,
  Withering beneath the fatal grasp.

Like a vapoury cloudlet is my heart,
  Growing into beauty near the sun,
Gaining rainbow hues in her embrace,
  Melting into tears when it is done.

Like mine own dear harp is this my heart,
  Dumb without the hand that sweeps its strings;
Though the hand be careless or be cruel,
  When it comes my heart breaks forth and sings.

ELIZABETH WORDSWORTH

(1840-1932)

Grandniece of William Wordsworth, she was born at Harrow, Middlesex, where her father, Christopher Wordsworth, later to become Bishop of Lincoln, was headmaster of Harrow School. She was educated at home according to strict religious principles. In 1878 she was appointed the first principal of Lady Margaret Hall, the Oxford women's college. For thirty years she made the College her life's work, gradually increasing its membership. In 1886, with a small legacy from her father, she founded another women's college, St Hugh's Hall, afterwards St Hugh's College. She received the honorary degrees of M.A. and D.C.L. and was made a Dame Commander of the British Empire.

Good and Clever

If all the good people were clever,
    And all clever people were good,
The world would be nicer than ever
    We thought that it possibly could.

But somehow 'tis seldom or never
    The two hit it off as they should;
The good are so harsh to the clever,
    The clever so rude to the good!

So, friends, let it be our endeavour
    To make each by each understood,
For few can be good like the clever,
    Or clever so well as the good!

The Great Frost, 1880-81

No roar of wheels is heard, no rush of feet;
    Grey gloomy sky hangs thick above our head,
Cold, hushed, and stiff in snowy winding-sheet
    Great London lies, as helpless as the dead,
    Like some famed empress, at whose long-watched bed
Physicians mark the heart's expiring beat,
And know nor gold nor skill can death defeat,
    Nor bring that ashen cheek one flush of red.
    Proud Queen of Cities, should this dreary hour
    Pass like a trance, and life's warm currents flow,
Say, wilt thou own the impotence of power,
    So seeming great, so suddenly laid low,
And raise one glance when storms have ceased to lower
    To Him who sends the sunshine and the snow?

January 1881

INDEX OF FIRST LINES